PRASE FOR *THE W.*

MW00780474

"Diana Paxson helps priests and priestesses give voice to the spirits with confidence. Not only does she reveal what seers do and how, she also restores the ancient and honored role of oracle to a questioning world."
> —CAITLÍN MATTHEWS, author of *Celtic Visions: Seership, Omens and Dreams of the Otherworld*

"Paxson makes a complex subject accessible. *The Way of the Oracle* will help readers hear the winds rustling the leaves of the sacred oak at Dodona. More importantly, it will help to keep prophesy from becoming a lost art."
> —EILEEN HOLLAND, author of *The Wicca Handbook* and *The Spellcaster's Reference*

"Reading a new book by Diana Paxson is entertainment coupled with scholarly information, with a twist of humor on top like a cherry on a cake. This book on the way of the oracles is yet another journey to remind us what we used to have, how humans can be in touch with more than just the visible world. We live in an invisible world as well, a mystery to most, but not to Diana. She has traveled over there many times, and she knows how to get out and, most importantly, how to get back. Mixed in are many real-life stories about how the Oracles worked their healing magic, and we begin to trust ourselves again—and that is a huge gift! Thanks Diana!"
> —Z. BUDAPEST, author of *Grandmother Moon*

"Gerald Gardner is considered to be the father of modern witchcraft, Michael Harner the father of modern shamanism. Diane Paxson, with the publication of this book, clearly places herself as the mother of modern trance-prophecy practice. With her other books on the subject, *The Way of the Oracle* is an essential primer for anyone interested in following the practices of Seidr, the Delphic Sibyl, or trance-prophecy in general. It is a book we will be happy to recommend to all of our students who practice this tradition."
> —JANET FARRAR AND GAVIN BONE, authors of *A Witches' Bible, The Witches' Goddess*, and *The Inner Mysteries*

"Diana Paxson is a writer of historical fantasy novels as well as an experienced seeress, skilled in the oracular arts and practices of her Nordic and Celtic ancestors. In this book she gives a fascinating account of these traditional arts, covering both the Nordic and Greek realms. Her meticulous scholarship and practical experience testing and working with the methods of the ancient *völvas* make this book a unique guide to these practices, which have a wide range of applicability in healing, problem solving, and spiritual guidance."
> —Ralph Metzner, PhD, psychologist and author of *The Well of Remembrance* and *Alchemical Divination*

"Diana Paxson is a pioneer in recovering oracular divination. She has a remarkable ability to draw from ancient sources from around the world to describe what seers did and still make seeing accessible and viable for a modern world. Paxson also presents a vast body of experience exploring this mysterious process. I worked as a seer with Paxson's Nordic seith group, her primary cultural focus. But I am also an academic folklorist, and an objective observer, and I am impressed by how she has used original sources, a deceptively simple method (trance and guided meditation), and her own lyrical poetry to weave a portal to another world where both the seer and seeker can discover knowledge to untangle the ordinary problems which confront us all. This is a wonderful introduction for the beginner, and a wealth of information for the trained oracle or scholar."
> —Dana Kramer-Rolls, social historian and folklorist, author of *The Way of the Cat*

"A fascinating journey into the oracular tradition: personal, profound, and enlightening."
> —Michelle Belanger, psychic/medium from A&E's *Paranormal State* and author of *The Psychic Energy Codex*

"As ever, Diana Paxson continues to make strong contributions to the Neopagan enterprise, grounding her suggestions and methods in a broad base of research in numerous Western traditions, augmenting her approach to altered states and ancient oracular techniques with a healthy respect for current trends in depth psychology and the neurosciences. Paxson's knowledge of myths, sagas, folk magic, and history is impressive and well matched by her considerable skills as an entertaining teacher and writer."
> —Erik D. Goodwyn, MD, author of *The Neurobiology of the Gods: How the Brain Shapes the Recurrent Imagery of Myth and Dreams*

THE WAY OF THE
ORACLE

THE WAY OF THE
ORACLE

Recovering the Practices of the Past to Find Answers for Today

DIANA L. PAXSON

WEISER BOOKS
San Francisco, CA / Newburyport, MA

First published in 2012 by Weiser Books
Red Wheel/Weiser, LLC
With offices at:
665 Third Street, Suite 400
San Francisco, CA 94107
www.redwheelweiser.com

ISBN: 978-1-57863-483-5

Library of Congress Cataloging-in-Publication Data is available upon request.

Cover design by Suzanne Albertson
Interior by Maureen Forys, Happenstance Type-O-Rama

Printed in the United States of America
TS
10 9 8 7 6 5 4 3 2 1

The paper used in this publication meets the minimum requirements of the American National Standard for Information Sciences—Permanence of Paper for Printed Library Materials Z39.48-1992 (R1997).

CONTENTS

ACKNOWLEDGMENTS

I have always found it easiest to learn in a group context, and I could not have developed this material without the cooperation, suggestions, and dedication of those who have worked with me in Seidhjallr, our working group in the San Francisco area, and participated in our training workshops.

I would especially like to recognize the contributions of Laurel Mendes, Lorrie Wood, Jordsvin, Winifred Hodge, Rod Landreth, Patricia Lafayllve, and the many others with whom I have worked over the years. Thanks also to Lorrie and Azi Vajravai for help with the music files. And finally, my thanks go to all those who have asked questions at oracle sessions from Berkeley to Britain. Without people who are looking for answers, there would be no oracle work at all.

INTRODUCTION

"A lot of help you are."

"But we are," said the calico koi. "We're just not supposed to do it directly. That's not part of being oracular. Our job is to make you think."

Diane Duane, *Wizards at War*

PANTHEACON, FEBRUARY 13, 2010

I sit in the high seat, pulling the veil down to hide my face, clasping my hands around the staff carved with the images of raven, cat, and bear. With doubled vision, I see the hotel function room, where sixty people are thinking about how to word their questions, and the mighty gate to Helheim, its timbers banded with iron and graven with runes of power. Outside, energy surges as the rest of the two thousand pagans who have come to Pantheacon continue to celebrate. But here we have created a warded place outside of time, and the way to wisdom is opening.

Passive, I wait as I have done so many times before, trusting my guide to watch over me, trusting the warders to take care of the people. The scene blurs, and I see a lantern-lit circle of redwood trees at an Ásatrú camp-out in Big Sur, torches and tall images at an Ár nDraíocht Féin: A Druid Fellowship (ADF) festival in Arizona, a green lawn beside a luminaria maze at Troth-moot in Indiana, the banner-hung walls of a Unitarian church in Berkeley, whispering trees in the Runestead at Brushwood in New York, a log building at a Covenant of the Goddess (CoG) Merrymeet in Washington, and a succession of workshop spaces and hotel function rooms, all transformed, like this one, by candlelight and song.

How many times have I sat here? How many questions have I answered since the night twenty years ago when I asked my circle of rune students if they would join me in learning how to do the work of an oracle for the pagan community. As always, I wonder if the magic will work, if I will be able to pass through the gate, if the visions will come. And as always, I remind myself that I am here to see for the people, and I make my will the offering.

"Seeress, thy way through the worlds thou must win . . . ," my guide begins to sing.

My eyes close. Responding to the music, awareness shifts, my breathing slows, and the outer world whirls away.

We begin.

IN SEARCH OF AN ORACLE

Everyone has questions, and in every human culture there have been those who sought for answers. Soothsayers, prophets, spae-wives, seers, and oracles are found throughout history. Today, psychics, intuitives, palm-readers, astrologers, and Tarot readers advertise everywhere.

But what do these people actually do?

The term "divination" comes from the Latin *divinare*, meaning "to foresee, to be inspired by a god," especially through the interpretation of omens. In earlier times, men sought omens in the flight of birds or the shapes of clouds or fire or the livers and other organs of sacrificed animals. Today, we use symbol systems, such as cards or lots or runes, or more direct means such as palmistry. In both divination and oracle work, the seer enters a trance state in which he or she receives information. The images that stimulate the diviner's perception are external, whereas the oracle receives information directly, derives it from images encountered internally, or channels the information from a higher power. Both approaches can provide useful counsel. Many books have been written on the art of reading cards, stars, and runes (including my own *Taking Up the Runes*). Fewer address the art of the oracle, and yet, throughout most of history, the oracles have been the most renowned.

The shaman also answers questions and gathers information by journeying in spirit to the Otherworld, using drumming and dancing to shift consciousness, while maintaining just enough connection to this world to control his body while participating in the vision. To get answers, shamans may look for a scene or image that sheds light on the question, or ask for information from his spirit allies or a being in the Otherworld. Shamans may also embody spirit beings, who then answer questions directly. All of this is very similar to the work of an oracle. Indeed, in *Nine Worlds of Seid-Magic,* Jenny Blain discusses *seidh* practices, including our oracular ritual, as examples of neo-shamanism. However, oracular practice has its own history.

Orestes, hounded by the Furies, asks the Pythoness at Delphi how to break their curse. Aeneas consults the Cumaean Sibyl regarding where he should lead the survivors of Troy. Queen Maeve asks the ban-filidh Fedelm what the result of the Cattle Raid of Cualigne will be. And in the *Saga of Erik the Red,* Thorbjorg, the "Little Völva," tells a gathering of anxious Greenlanders when the famine will end. Such literary episodes reflect the practices and beliefs of their times. But people have similar questions today. They want to talk to their lost loved ones, heal old family traumas, and find out about work, projects, and prospects. Now, as then, the uncertainties of life drive people to seek information on everything from love to livelihood.

But what can oracles actually predict? To accurately foretell the future assumes a deterministic universe in which fate or some higher power has already decided what *will* be. If knowing what is going to happen does not allow you to change it, why bother to ask? I prefer to believe in probability rather than predestination, and I choose to act as though my decisions can make a difference. I believe that the role of the oracle is not to declare what *must* be, but to identify probabilities and clarify the questioner's choices in a way he or she can understand.

Just as some people are born with perfect pitch or the hand-eye coordination of the artist, for some, seeing possible outcomes may be only too easy. The agonies of the unwilling prophet are a staple of literature. And yet, like manual dexterity and singing, perceiving probabilities is a basic human ability. In this book, we will see how this ability can be trained and used.

The methods presented in Part Two build on the basic trance skills laid out in my earlier book, *Trance-Portation.* Improving communication between your unconscious and conscious minds brings self-knowledge and helps you make decisions. Oracle work is a unique and rewarding experience, in which exploring the potential of other minds expands our own. It brings us into contact with spirits, human and other. Seeking answers, we range through the inner worlds.

BIOGRAPHY

My own oracular journey started in the eighties, when I was simultaneously beginning a career as a writer of fiction and becoming a priestess. While researching *Brisingamen,* a novel based on Norse mythology, I encountered descriptions of the Viking Age magic called *seidh,* which included an oracular ritual, and wondered if this skill could be practiced in the modern world.

The core shamanic techniques described in Michael Harner's *The Way of the Shaman* fit well into the array of skills I was developing, but I felt the need for a more culturally embedded tradition. On the other hand, I was not willing to immerse myself in the culture of any of the indigenous peoples who were then being proclaimed as the only authentic sources for shamanic practice.

In 1987, I was able to take Harner's "Basic Workshop." I came to the workshop hoping for help in recovering the shamanistic skills of my own Northern European ancestors. When, on the second day, Harner announced that we would be journeying to the Upper World to find a teacher in human form, the figure I encountered was the Norse god Odin. That was the beginning of a continuing relationship. The rune study with which I began my exploration of Germanic culture is presented in *Taking Up the Runes,* but that was only the prequel to an effort to reconstruct northern oracular practice—an effort that continues to this day.

To fill in the gaps in the Norse seidh lore, I have explored oracular practices wherever I could find them. Thus, although a great deal of the material in this book will be drawn from the Germanic tradition, what I am presenting in Part Two might be termed a "Core Oracular Practice" drawn from the prophetic literature of many lands, whose principles can be used to retro-engineer oracle work within a variety of traditions. The pythias at Delphi and the völvas of early Scandinavia had the support of a trained team, but many seers in the past worked alone, giving responses spontaneously rather than in the context of ritual. By analyzing both communal and solo oracular practices, we can identify the basic skills and process and explore ways to incorporate them into individual and community practice today.

Since the beginning, my purpose has been not only to serve my local community, but also to introduce oracular practice to a wider audience. In the mid-nineties, I began to conduct workshops, and a number of individuals and groups using or influenced by these techniques are working in the United States and Europe today.

I and my group are not the only ones who do this work, and our approach is not the only one that can succeed; otherwise, although the historical information on the work of an oracle might be of interest, there would be no point in sharing what we have learned. My hope is that this book will encourage readers who feel the call to improve their own oracular intuition and to serve their communities to develop their own variations on a practice that can be immensely rewarding both to those who ask questions and those who answer.

Part One

IN SEARCH OF THE ORACLE

I

SEERS AND SPEAKERS: THE SELECTION, TRAINING, AND ROLE OF AN ORACLE

Then I take, as prophetess, my place and seat.
And this time may (the gods) bless the going-in much more than ever before,
Both to me and to all from Hellas who are admitted,
As the custom is, by fall of the lot;
For I give response according as the god may lead.

Eumenides, Act I

King Aegeus consults the oracle at Delphi, Attic red-figured Kylix by the Kodros painter, Antikensammlung Museum, Berlin

"What is your name?" Medb said to the girl.

"I am Fedelm, and I am a womanpoet [banfáid] of Connacht."

"Where have you come from?" Medb said.

"From learning verse and vision [filidecht] in Alba," the girl said.

"Have you the imbas forosnai, the Light of Foresight?" Medb said.

"Yes I have," the girl said.

"Then look for me and see what will become of my army."

So the girl looked.

Tain Bo Cuailnge II

And now many things are revealed to me which were before hidden from me and others. I can now say that the famine will not last much longer, and that conditions will improve with the spring; and the epidemic which has persisted for so long will abate sooner than expected. And as for you, Gudrid, I shall reward you at once for the help you have given us, for I can see your whole fate [forlög] with great clarity now. . . .

Saga of Erik the Red 4

I see two things. They are related. I see a small creek high in the mountain, fresh melting snow. The first crocus raises her head, stretches open to the sun. The rune with this is Jera. We are coming out of the dark side of the year. Like the crocus you are sprouting but have not yet budded open. Give it time, trust in the sun, and let yourself be tickled, or healed.

Answer 13 from Seidh session,
January 11, 2005, Berkeley, California

Since humans first became self-aware, we've sought to understand the forces that shape our lives. The scientist collects data to predict the probability of events; the farmer uses experience to decide when to harvest. But when ordinary sources of information fail, men seek guidance by other means. Throughout history, some people have had a talent for giving advice and making predictions. The pythia at Delphi, the Irish druidess, the Greenland völva, and the modern seer are all called to serve as oracles. But who are they? How did they come to their calling, and how do they answer questions?

WHAT'S IN A NAME?

Oracular practitioners come in both genders. Except when a female is specified, throughout this book, the term "seer" will be used for both. Although words such as "oracle" or "prophet" are often used to mean someone who prognosticates future events, the terms themselves have a broader meaning, derived from roots meaning "to speak" or "to see." Whichever element is foremost, both must be present. The mystic may or may not communicate his experiences; the oracle must do so. The word "oracle" itself comes from the Latin *oraculum*, "to speak," and can refer to the person who channels information or instructions or to the place in which the answers are given.

In Greek, the word for a seer or soothsayer is *mantis*. A "prophet," from the Greek *prophētēs* (from *pro* "for" and *phanai* "to speak"), utters divine revelations or foretells future events. A "seer" or "seeress" is someone who has extraordinary moral and spiritual insights, and whose information comes in the form of visions. In the ancient Mediterranean, we find the Latin *sibyl*, a title given to a number of legendary prophetesses, especially the Sibyl of Cumae, and the Pythia, or Pythoness, a title derived from the serpent who once guarded the Delphic shrine.

In Viking Age Scandinavia, the *spákona/spaewife* (a woman) and the *spámadhr* (a man) entered a trance state and "spoke" answers. Oracular trance was also among the magical skills of the wisewoman called the *völva*, while the *thul* (Old Norse) or *thyle* (Old English) was a "speaker." The term *uatis*, or *ovateis* (modernized as "ovate"), was used by Strabo (*Geographia* IV, 4) for the Gaulish priestly class that included diviners and natural philosophers. In early Ireland, one of the skills that the *filidh*, the druidic poet, was expected to master was prophecy. In Ireland, a male seer was called a *fáith*, and in Britain, an *offydd*. In the selection from the *Tain*, we meet a female seer, Fedelm the *banfáid*.

THE ROLE OF THE ORACLE

To reconstruct oracular practice, we need to understand not only who the seers were, but also what they did. The seer perceived an answer directly and delivered it in his or her own words, while the prophet channeled or was possessed by a deity, but the kinds of questions they answered were essentially the same. The oracles responded both to individual needs and community concerns, providing counsel and consolation in times of prosperity and uncertainty. They do the same today.

THE MYSTIQUE OF DELPHI

From the earliest times, we find mention of prophets and oracles in the Mediterranean world. One of them is Cassandra, a Trojan princess who was a temple seer before she refused Apollo's attentions and was cursed to utter prophecies that no one would believe. Even more interesting is Tiresias, a prophet of Thebes. In the *Bacchae* of Euripides, he tries to warn King Pentheus that he must accept the new cult of Dionysos. In Sophocles' *Oedipus Rex,* he unwillingly reveals to King Oedipus that the young king's own inadvertent sin is the cause of the plague currently threatening the town. The prophecies come from Delphi, but it is Tiresias who interprets them.

Although Delphi seems to have been an oracular center as early as the Mycenean period, its great fame developed after the Dorian migration into Hellas and the Peloponnese, when it was taken over by the cult of Apollo and endured for a thousand years. As Dempsey puts it in his comprehensive and enthusiastic survey of the influence of the Delphic oracle,

> Greek and barbarian alike consulted it: envoys came from Asia and Libya and distant Italy seeking advice on all matters of moment. The framing of laws, the founding of colonies, the making and unmaking of kings, the beginning of wars, the healing of disease or pestilence—these and such-like questions were submitted to the unerring judgment of the omniscient Apollo. From the earliest times the Oracle of Delphi influenced the history of noble houses, aye, and of whole nations. The Delphic Oracle of Apollo, as no other oracle of antiquity, long inspired a living faith, and for centuries retained its credit unimpaired. (Dempsey 1918, 39)

One reason for this popularity may have been its location, for although its impressive setting on the slope below Mount Parnassus requires a climb, the area is accessible from both the north and east and the Peloponnese. As its reputation grew, the many rich gifts with which grateful questioners adorned it would have added to its appeal, and it didn't hurt that

Pindar, one of the most renowned of the Greek poets, was a devotee. Still, none of that would have mattered if the seeresses had not established an enviable track record of useful answers and a reputation for integrity.

As we shall see in the discussion of oracular answers in Chapter IV, many of the questions were personal. However, a fair proportion of the recorded answers were given to cities whose questions affected the whole community. Even Apollo could not impose political unity on the Greeks, but his answers helped to create a consensus regarding religion. Nor was prophecy all the site had to offer. Delphi hosted numerous festivals and the Pythian Games, which featured artistic as well as athletic competitions.

During the first centuries of the Roman Empire, another important site was the great temple of Apollo at Claros, on what is now the coast of Turkey. Visitors inscribed their names, origin, and the dates of their visits on the marble blocks of the sanctuary. Where pilgrims from mainland Greece visited Delphi, Claros served clients from all over the Near East. Though the prophet here was male, the answers were very similar to those given at Delphi.

BARDS AND OVATES

The Druid order was divided into three specialties: the bards, the ovates (variously given as *uatis* or *euhages/orates)*, and those druids who were mystics and philosophers. In later Irish lore, the bards serve as seers. The Classical sources indicate that the druids also served as judges and arbiters. According to Diogenes Laertius, the Druids, "make their pronouncements by means of riddles and dark sayings, teaching that the gods must be worshipped, and no evil done, and manly behaviour maintained." (*Vitae* I:5, introduction, in Matthews 1996, 20), which sounds like the kind of response given by an oracle. Female druids are said to have given impromptu prophecies to the future Roman emperors Diocletian and Aurelian. Among the officers required to attend upon King Cormac was a druid, "to offer sacrifices, and to forebode good or evil to the country by means of his skill and magic . . ." (Keating, in Matthews 1996).

In addition to the divination accomplished as part of a ritual or sacrifice or through the interpretation of auguries, the druids were noted for spontaneous prophecies, and it is these that we find most often in the tales. In the eighth-century *Compert Conchoboir*, we find an impromptu prophecy by the druid Cathbad. The king's daughter Nes asks, "What is the present hour lucky for?" "For begetting a king on a queen," he replies. Seeing no other man nearby, she takes him inside, and nine months later she gives birth to Conchobar, the king who will later command Cuchulain in the *Tain Bo Cuailgne*. Cathbad also foretells that the newborn Dierdre will bring great misfortune and mischief to the kingdom.

In another early tale, the warrior-woman Scáthach uses the *imbas forosnai* ("the light of foresight") to chant a long poem foretelling Cuchulain's future. As seen in the quotes at the beginning of this chapter, the *ban-fáith* Fedelm also uses the *imbas forasnai* to answer Maeve's question about the outcome of the war against Ulster.

GERMANIC SEERS

In the histories of Tacitus, we learn that during the first century the Germans honored a seeress called Veleda,

> a maiden of the tribe of the Bructeri, who possessed extensive dominion; for by ancient usage the Germans attributed to many of their women prophetic powers and, as the superstition grew in strength, even actual divinity. The authority of Veleda was then at its height, because she had foretold the success of the Germans and the destruction of the legions. (*Histories* IV, 61)

She is said to have lived by the Lippe River on the German side of the Rhine, but she was influential throughout central Germany. When the Batavian chieftain Civilis rebelled against Rome, she became his chief advisor. Like the seers of the Mediterranean, Veleda stayed in one place, where she received questioners, and her answers, like theirs, determined the fate of nations.

The Viking Age völva operated on a smaller scale and moved from place to place rather than requiring querents to come to her. Chapter 4 of the *Saga of Erik the Red* describes an oracular ritual at a farmstead in Greenland:

> A woman named Thorbjorg was in the settlement. She was a prophetess [*spákona*] and called the "Little Völva." She had nine sisters,

all of whom were prophetesses *[spákonur]*. She was the only one left alive. It was Thorbjorg's custom to go to feasts in the winter, and people invited her to their homes most who wanted foreknowledge of their destiny *[forlög]*, or that of the season.

The situation was similar in mainland Scandinavia. In *Nornageststhattr* 11, Gestr tells King Olaf that when he was born, "Völvur were travelling around the countryside. They were called spákonur, and they prophesied men's fates. Therefore people gave them lodgings and prepared feasts for them and gave them gifts upon their departure. My father did this too, and they came to his place with their entourage." We find similar descriptions in the *Arrow-Odd's Saga* 2 and the *Saga of Olaf Tryggvason* in the *Flateyjarbók*.

It would appear that whereas each area of the Mediterranean world had its permanent oracular site, in the North, a seidh-group would operate in each region, moving from the steading of one jarl or prosperous farmer to another to answer questions of general importance, such as the prospects for a good harvest, and personal interest, such as marriage.

THE CALLED AND THE CHOSEN

Where did (and do) these seers and prophets come from, and how did they learn their craft?

Many assume that psychic sensitivity, like perfect pitch or the ability to draw, is inborn. While some individuals have innate abilities in these areas, even the born genius will not make effective use of them without training and discipline, and the gifts of the natural psychic can be a curse if they are not trained. But talent, in any field, is not an either-or matter. In *Trance-Portation*, I presented a sequence of exercises to develop the controlled ability to do trance work. These basic disciplines can be directed to specific applications, such as oracular practice. Changing one's state of consciousness is an innate human ability. Just as those of moderate talent can be taught to make music or paint, many, with the proper support and training, can achieve a state in which they can answer questions with a deeper wisdom than they have while in an ordinary state of mind.

Both independent and community-supported oracles have served their people well. In general, prophets who function independently and spontaneously have a great deal of natural talent and/or long and intensive training behind them. On the other hand, a good support team and a powerful ritual can enable a less-experienced seer to serve.

The Mediterranean

Prophets are a common figure in Greek legend. According to Hesiod, Tiresias of Thebes made the mistake of disturbing a pair of copulating snakes and was punished by Hera with transformation into a woman, in which shape he married and had children, including a daughter called Manto (meaning "prophecy"). After seven years, he encountered another pair of snakes, guarded them, and was changed back again. However, when Zeus and Hera asked him to give evidence regarding whether men or women got more pleasure from sex, he agreed with Zeus that women got more and was struck blind by Hera. In compensation, Zeus gave him the gift of foresight and the life span of seven men.

As a two-sexed ecstatic with serpent connections, Tiresias has a shamanic aspect to his character. He prophesies to Odysseus in the land of the dead and, in the Classical Greek plays, uses a number of prophetic techniques, including vision, augury from the songs of birds, and interpretation of images in the smoke of burnt offerings. His prophecies are usually enigmatic, and only after the tragic conclusion does their meaning become clear.

The priests and priestesses who served the oracles in the Classical period, on the other hand, were virtually anonymous, leaving the emphasis on the ritual and setting. Those we know of were local people from families that had served the oracle for generations. The most famous are the pythias of Delphi. What we know of their lives is culled from a variety of Classical sources, especially the writings of Plutarch, who served as a priest at Delphi for a time.

The pythias had to be freeborn citizens of the town. In an institution that lasted over a thousand years, there were inevitably changes. The early oracular priestesses were apparently required to be maidens, but after a querent attempted to seduce the pythia, the priestesses were chosen from among the postmenopausal women of good character, who were presumably less susceptible. According to Diodorus, however, they dressed in the style of a maiden. Plutarch tells us that she who now serves the God has been born as respectably as any man here, and has lived as good and orderly a life; but having been reared in the house of small farmer folk, she brings nothing with her from art or from practice or faculty whatsoever, as she goes down into the sanctuary. As Xenophon thinks that the bride should step into her husband's home having seen as little as may be, and heard as little, so she, ignorant and untried in almost all things, and a true virgin in soul, is associated with the God. (*Pythia* XXII)

If, as Plutarch tells us, the priestess was neither educated nor a born psychic, how was she able to function as an oracle? In his essay on the decline of oracles, Plutarch stated his belief that it was the energies of the oracular site itself, whether they were the mysterious hallucinogenic vapors whose existence has been so often debated, or one of the many "potencies" sent forth by the earth, that altered the pythia's consciousness.

What he does not take into account is the fact that the pythia would have been brought up on stories about the oracle. Delphi received visitors from all over the world, and even its women would have had a relatively sophisticated knowledge of current affairs. The protections with which the pythia was surrounded would aid her in maintaining calmness and clarity. Even without the assistance of narcotic vapors, the expectation of a change in consciousness, the visual cues, and the ritual preparations and procedure would work together to put the priestess into a prophetic trance.

But Delphi was not the only place of prophecy. During the first through third centuries, the oracle of Apollo at Claros was nearly as prestigious. Unlike the pythias, the priests who gave the Claros oracles served for a term and then returned to ordinary life, but they did prepare for each session by withdrawing from the world for a day and a night of prayer and fasting. Tacitus tells us that

[t]here, it is not a woman, as at Delphi, but a priest chosen from certain families, generally from Miletus, who ascertains simply the number and the names of the applicants. Then descending into a cave and drinking a draught from a secret spring, the man, who is commonly ignorant of letters and of poetry, utters a response in verse

answering to the thoughts conceived in the mind of any inquirer. It was said that he prophesied to Germanicus, in dark hints, as oracles usually do, an early doom. (*Histories* II, 54)

The Celtic World

The first Roman writers to encounter the Celts noted that the Druid priests underwent an intensive training. According to Caesar, "many resort to their school even of their own accord, whilst others are sent by their parents and relations. There they are said to learn thoroughly a great number of verses. On that account, some continue at their education for twenty years" (*Bello Gallico* VI, 13, in Matthews 1996, 16).

In the later period, seership survived as a poetic function. Our information regarding the training of the Celtic *fili* comes mainly from the Old Irish literature, in particular the *Glossary of Cormac* and the Metrical Tractates. Nothing in Celtic literature is ever stated clearly. The surviving accounts sometimes contradict each other and were, in any case, written down in Christian times when some of the knowledge had been lost. There is a general agreement that among the fourteen poetic skills mastered by a fili were three that enabled him to prophesy: the *imbas forosnai, tenm laida,* and *dichetal do chennaib na tuaithe,* respectively translated by Kuno Meyer as "illumination of song," "knowledge which illuminates," and "extempore incantation" (Meyer, in Matthews 1999, 49).

In some accounts, prophecy was delivered within the context of a mantic ritual in which the seer lay in a certain position, or covered his eyes, or first made offerings or chewed on his thumb. These rituals will be discussed further in Chapter IV. In other sources, the fili utters his or her pronouncements without preparation in response to a question, developing them in the form of a poem or song.

Extemporaneous prophecy is certainly the pattern we find in later Celtic folklore, in which the Sight can be stimulated in those who are so gifted in response to things seen or heard, as well as in answer to a question. In the older stories, the power usually comes from an Otherworldly source. It is said that the Welsh bard Taliesin was in a previous incarnation the boy Gwion Bach, who was set to stir the cauldron in which the goddess Ceridwen was brewing a potion that would grant *awen*—wisdom and inspiration. When it splattered, he sucked from his thumb the magical first three drops. We find a similar tale in *The Boyhood Days of Fionn*. Fionn MacCumhal studied with the druid Finegas to learn the art of poetry, but it was only when he inadvertently touched the roasting Salmon of Wisdom and licked his burnt thumb that he received the full power the salmon had absorbed from eating magical hazelnuts, which had fallen into the pool of prophecy at the source of the Boyne. In another and possibly earlier story, Fionn gained the power when his thumb got smashed in the door of a fairy mound.

Scandinavia

References to seers who speak as oracles are abundant in the lore of the Viking Age. There is, however, some debate about what their practice should be called. In *Ynglingasaga* 7, we learn that "Odin knew and practised that craft which brought most power and which was called *seidh* (witchcraft), and he therefore knew much of man's fate and of the future." Since forecasting the future and telling people their fates is exactly what the völvas are described as doing in a multitude of episodes in the sagas, it is clear that oracle work is among the practices included under the heading of seidh, but it is not the only form of magic described under this name. In the accounts, the terms *seidh* and *spá* (modern "spae") are used interchangeably, as are the various names for those who speak prophecy. Because some of the references to seidh describe negative magic, there is some prejudice against the term; however, it is also the best known. For this reason, I refer to Norse oracular practice both as "Oracular Seidh" and "spae."

In the *Shorter Seeress' Prophecy* 6, we are told that the seeresses [*völvur*] came from Viðolfr, the magicians [*vitkar*] from Vilmeiðr, and the soothsayers [*seidhberendur*] from Svarthöfdi. These are the names of giants, the implication being that like the norns, who are their Otherworldly analogue, people who worked magic, including the giving of prophecies, are literally or spiritually descended from the primal powers. I think, however, that this must be taken metaphorically, as the seers mentioned in the sagas, like the one in *Hrolf Kraki's Saga* who tried to change her prophecy when King Frodhi threatened to torture her, are clearly human beings.

A common belief that the folk of Finland (especially the Saami) were skilled in magic persisted through the Middle Ages. "A Finnish woman" is the seeress in *Vatnsdaelasaga* 10, and in the *History of Harald Hairfair*

33, Eric Bloodaxe meets Gunhild, who becomes his queen and a famous sorceress, in Finmark, where she has come "to learn seidh from the two Finns who are the cleverest men in Finmark." However, it is unlikely that all of the women and men who worked seidh came from Finland.

I believe that a more probable explanation for the origin of the seers may be found in the sagas. The völva Thorbjorg who answers questions in the *Saga of Erik the Red* is said to be the only survivor of a group of nine "sisters." In *Arrow-Odd's Saga 2*, there is a description of a seidh session in which the seeress is

> [a] woman was named Heidh. She was a seeress *[völva]* and sorceress *[seidhkona]* and she knew unspoken things by means of her knowledge *[frodhleikr]*. She travelled widely to feasts, to which farmers invited her, throughout the land. She told people their fates *[ørlög]* and forecast the weather for the coming winter or other things. She had thirty people with her, fifteen boys and fifteen girls. They were great reciters, as was she.

From this passage, we know that the spae ritual involved singing, which we will discuss in more detail in Chapters II and V. We also see that the rituals originally involved men as well as women. Although we are not told that they practiced prophecy, in the *History of Harald Hairfair* 25, 35, we learn that Ragnar Rettilbone and his eighty *seidhmenn* lived together in Hadeland and practiced seidh. He was a son of Harald Hairfair by the beautiful daughter of a Finn living in Norway, but perhaps because he had once loved her too madly, in his later years, King Harald banned seidh. When another seidhmadhr objected on the grounds that one of the king's sons was practicing magic, Harald instructed his favorite son, Eric Bloodaxe, to deal with the situation, which he did by burning his brother and his eighty companions to death in their hall.

Although we have no specific information on their training, we can guess that *seidhberendr* learned the various skills involved in their craft, including spae, from older practitioners. One can imagine these groups touring the country, led by one or more experienced völvas or spámadhrs. In the ritual, they would raise energy through singing and serve their leader in exchange for the opportunity to learn. Those who proved to have talent would eventually become seers in turn. By the time Erik the Red settled in Greenland, encroaching Christianity was bringing the old ways into disrepute, and parents were not sending their children to learn sorcery. Thus, Thorbjorg was the last of her kind.

BECOMING A SEER TODAY

As a child, I was very vulnerable. To protect myself, at an early age I developed such good mental shields that by the time I was grown I believed I had no psychic ability at all. Recovering those abilities took many years. I first encountered information about northern European oracular practices in H. R. Ellis Davidson's *Gods and Myths of the Viking Age,* and I have been learning ever since. Since I began doing public work in 1991 I have taught many workshops, and the idea has spread. In preparing this book, I questioned many contemporary seers, both those who have taken my workshops and those who have learned oracular practice independently. Here are some of their replies.

> I was taught to do this as part of a family magical practice. Because I was the daughter born to the right part of a certain bloodline, it was my job. It started slowly and is part of a bigger practice. I was taught in stages and through many different processes; for example, some of it was taught by beings I call Fae.
>
> Nanette Boyster

> I worked alone for about four or five years, starting with Michael Harner's guidelines from his book The Way of the Shaman and taking off on my own from there. In 1995, I took a class with Diana Paxson and Laurel Olsen and established a more Heathen-oriented and community-service approach. Before the class, my work had been for personal religious and psychological development, skills development, and otherworldly exploration. After the class, my work became more oriented toward Heathen community service, including serving Heathen folk and departed kin and friends, and having contact with the holy ones for the sake of others as well as myself.
>
> Winifred Hodge

> In February 1997, after enough encounters with the runes to interest me in them as a divination technique and magical toolset, I had

a significant experience while watching Hrafnar's *seið* group (since named Seiðhjallr) perform their oracular *seið* ritual. In turn, this led me to seek out their method of oracular practice and learn it. Some years later, they allowed me to join the team.

Lorrie Wood

From the preceding accounts, it should be apparent that although some seers are born and some are chosen, it is also a skill that can be acquired with the proper training. The call to serve the people by conveying divine wisdom is still heard today.

Although many of those reading this book will simply be seeking more information about oracles and prophetic practices, some of you have heard that call. The exercises in Part Two of this book are intended to help you answer it.

II

PSYCHE AND SETTING: ORACULAR SITES AND SPIRITS

In the hour between day and darkness, doorways open between the worlds. Beneath the rocky height of Cumae, the darkness deepens. The track you follow leads to a cleft that's darker still. Behind you, Lake Avernus gleams from its crater, hiding the gateway to the Otherworld. To find it, you need information. But the Sibyl's cave may prove even more perilous.

Entrance to the Antro Sibylla, Cumae

The ground quivers beneath your feet. You cling to a slender oak tree until the tremors cease, nose twitching at the whiff of sulfur. Crimson poppies are scattered like drops of blood upon the grass, and silvery artemisia stars the open hillside. Eastward the sky flickers red, and you know that Vesuvius is wakening. This is a fair land, but filled with unexpected dangers.

Two outcrops of sandy golden rock show through the trees, framing a dark opening, drawing you in. A breath of chill air flows from the strange, trapezoid-shaped cleft beyond. You shiver, but you stand your ground—you have not endured so many perils to run away.

You reach out with all your senses, seeking the power that dwells within these caves. And wind, blasting suddenly from the myriad apertures in the stone, howls around you. You cry out the question that weighs upon your soul, and the Sibyl, speaking with a hundred voices, answers you.

In 1998, I had the good fortune to climb the path to the "Antro Sibylla" at Cumae, where the oracle showed Aeneas the way to the Underworld. My visit took place in the brightness of noon, without vapors, signs, or portents. But simply being in such a dramatic setting was enough to open my awareness. Since Naples is home to a major NATO base, my mind was full of the war going on just across the Adriatic. I leaned against the cool, mineral-stained stone, pen and notebook in hand, and this is what I heard:

I am a voice of wind . . .
I am a voice of fire . . .
I am the voice of the eternal stone . . .
and I speak with the voice of the sea.
Open thine ears, and I will prophesy
of the movements of earth and of nations.
The harpies scream above Dacia;
Beware the Dragon who will arise in wrath and fire;
Let the Eagle beware, and let the Bear flee also;
This fight is for neither.
It is a brood of serpents who tangle and fight.
Only Medusa can turn them against each other
and so stop the war. . . .

Most of the imagery was obvious, although I figured out the identity of the Dragon only after the bombing of the Chinese embassy. The oracle had been long deserted, but she was speaking still.

For a seer who is well trained and willing, or naturally very open, the question alone may be a sufficient stimulus, but the elaborate oracular establishments of the ancient world suggest that getting answers is easier if the process is supported by an appropriate setting. An external setting is a physical location in which an oracle works; an internal setting is an inner landscape featuring associated imagery. An ascent or descent to a hidden place with a well or spring and a sacred tree or trees are found in too many oracular contexts to be chance. They are part of the psychic environment of the oracular state, which can be reached more easily by invoking them.

ORACULAR SITES IN THE ANCIENT WORLD

In the Mediterranean world, oracles were associated with specific sites, and many elements of those sites are also familiar from the northern legend. What can these sites tell us about the archetypal landscape of prophecy?

Dodona

The oldest oracle was said to be the one in Dodona, near Ioannina in northern Greece—a wild, mountainous, and isolated region even today. It had been in use since the Mycenean Age. The original deity seems to have been Dione, whose name means simply "goddess" and is cognate to "Dias," the early form of the name of her consort, Zeus, who was worshipped with her as the god of the sacred spring. The oracle was served by priests called the Selloi, who heard the answers to questions in the rustling of the wind in the leaves, or priestesses called *peleaides*, "doves," who interpreted the cooing of the birds that lived in the sacred oak or beech trees.

Claros

One of the most famous oracles was located at Claros, in a valley on the coast of what is now Turkey. It was in use as early as the ninth century BCE, but it was not until the Roman period that it reached the height of its fame. Travelers approached through a series of three gates, beyond which lay the sacred grove and the temple of Apollo. Oracles were given at night in an underground chamber, which could be entered only by creeping through a thirty-yard passageway faced with blue marble, with seven turnings. Questioners sat in an outer chamber, where they could contemplate the omphalos stone, representing the navel of the world, while the oracular priest and the thespode continued on to the inner chamber that surrounded the spring. The priest, already prepared by meditation and fasting, drank from the sacred spring and went into a trance in which he spoke words that were translated into poetry by the thespode. When the answer had been given, clients and priests would return through a second passageway to the temple.

Cumae and Others

The Antro Sibylla, described at the beginning of this chapter, is the site identified by tradition as the home of the Sibyl of Cumae. It is located near the Bay of Naples, on a knob of rock that stands between Lake Avernus and the Tyrrhenian Sea, one of the few stable points in an area that is prone to sudden changes in elevation and the occasional eruption from Mt. Vesuvius. At times, vents on the hillsides or beneath the lake emit sulfurous fumes. The knob itself was first settled by Greek colonists in the eighth century BCE. The summit is crowned by the ruins of a temple to Apollo. Farther down, a strange, trapezoidal tunnel, identified as the Sibyl's "cave," runs beneath the hillside. This is how Virgil presents it in the *Aeneid* VI, 60–64:

> *The giant flank of that Euboean crag*
> *has been dug out into a cave; a hundred*
> *broad ways lead to that place, a hundred gates;*
> *as many voices rush from these—the Sibyl's*
> *replies . . .*

The "hundred gates" may refer to the windows cut from the tunnel through the side of the hill. As I found when I visited in 1998, the literary associations are enough to inspire the spirit of prophecy. But by the time Virgil wrote, the Sibyl of Cumae had been silent for centuries. It is not even certain that the tunnel/cave was the site of the oracle. The Romans believed the Sibyl to be an oracle of Apollo, but a votive pit from the early Greek period yielded a clay disc inscribed with "Hera does not permit you to return and consult the oracle again." The clay disc may indicate that oracles were drawn, rather than channeled, or the disc may be a record made after the oracle was received.

In the *Aeneid*, the hero reaches the Underworld through a

> *wide-mouthed cavern, deep and vast*
> *and rugged, sheltered by a shadowed lake*
> *and darkened groves; such vapor poured from these*
> *black jaws to heaven's vault; no bird could fly*
> *above unharmed.* . . . (*Aeneid* VI, 318–321)

If there was once such a cavern by Lake Avernus, it is no longer visible; however, at the Bay of Baiae nearby there is a less-known location at which the living may have communicated with the dead. This site consisted of a series of underground tunnels that recreated the topography of the Greek Underworld, including a boiling river identified with the Styx, which querents crossed in a boat, and culminating in an underground chamber in which, their minds prepared by the terrors of their journey, they presumably asked their questions. The oracle and its activities were described by the Roman author Strabo. Closed down during the reign of Emperor Augustus in the first century CE, its existence was suppressed and its location lost until it was rediscovered by Robert Paget in 1962. It was not until 2001 that Robert Temple was able to explore and describe the site more fully.

Temple also describes a similar complex, the Nekromanteion at Thesprotia, in Greece, which has been fully excavated and analyzed. Located amidst mountains and gorges, it is approached by a river named after the Acheron found in Hades. The consultation chamber was underground. The questioner underwent purification and ate a special diet, which may have had a trance-producing effect. After pouring libations and sacrificing a pig, he made his way through labyrinthine passageways to a chamber where he confronted the images of the dead and presumably heard their words. How exactly this was accomplished—whether the priests of the shrine answered on behalf of the dead, or the querent was sufficiently entranced by the setting and possibly by drugs to hear the voices directly—is still open to speculation.

Delphi

The most famous of the ancient oracles was the one at Delphi, on the slopes of Mount Parnassus, above the Corinthian Gulf. Although its location is geographically central, getting to the actual site, terraced into a spur jutting from the side of the mountain above a spectacular gorge, involves a tortuous ascent. However, the effort is as worthwhile today as it was in ancient times. The waters that fed the sacred spring called the Cassotis, which once flowed to the temple, have been diverted to provide water to the town of Delphi, but the Castalian Spring at which pilgrims were purified still produces a constant flow of cold pure water. The nearby museum holds an impressive selection of the statuary that once adorned the sanctuary. From the Neolithic period to 395 CE, when Emperor Theodosius shut it down, Delphi was home to the most prestigious oracle of all.

Model of Ancient Delphi, Delphi Museum

According to the myths, the potential of the site was discovered when some goats became drunk on vapors issuing from fissures in the earth. Although later poets derived its name from the dolphin, in whose form Apollo carried the first priests of his temple there, it probably actually comes from the same root as *delphys*, "womb." This would make sense, as there is considerable evidence that it was originally sacred to Gaia, the goddess of earth, as we know from the opening words of the seeress in *The Eumenides* I, i:

> First for my prayer: whereby I give precedence among gods to the first giver of oracles, Earth; and after her to Themis, who came second to this oracular seat, her mother's with good right; and at the

third succession, with consent of Themis and without violence to any, one Titan-born, she too Earth's child, took the seat—Phoebe, who gave it for a birth-gift to Phoebus (Apollo).

The omphalos stone, the navel stone of the world, was one of its greatest treasures. The site was also called Pytho, in recognition of the serpent, a daughter of Gaia, who guarded it. Poseidon Earthshaker at one time had an altar there. Apollo's presence was also explained by a later story in which he killed the python because it had tried to harm his mother when she was pregnant with him, after which he took over the shrine.

The place from which the fumes emerged was surrounded by a temple, which was built and rebuilt over the centuries. The temple of Apollo, whose foundations and pillars can be seen today, dates from the fourth century BCE. Like everything else at Delphi, it is set into the hillside. The *adyton,* the oracular chamber at the western end of the building, is about nine by sixteen feet in size and set into the crypt below. Today that area has been backfilled with earth, so even if visitors were allowed to climb on the ruins, it would not be possible to enter it. However, there is a niche in the outer face on the southern side of the foundations in which you can sit and where the god may speak to you.

Everyone involved in consulting the oracle began by purifying themselves at the Castalian Spring. From there, the priestess processed up to drink from the Cassotis, which had been channeled into a basin just above and in front of the temple. Pausanias tells us that its water "makes women prophetic in the god's holy places" (I:X:24[5]). Originally it seems to have run under the temple, but when a landslide changed the water table, it was piped in through a series of channels. A block of limestone with indentations suggests that water might have been channeled around the tripod on which the seeress sat (Temple 2005, 99).

If the omens indicated that questions could be asked, the priestess entered the sanctuary, which held the most holy objects, including the omphalos stone, the grave of Dionysos, and possibly a statue of Apollo. If intoxicating vapors did indeed filter up through the earthen floor, this is where they would have emerged. Here, also, was the tripod, a concave platter supported by three pillars. In a multitude of images on vases and elsewhere, we see the seeress sitting on the tripod to prophesy, holding a branch of laurel in one hand and in the other a bowl of water. Querents waited in a separate, adjoining area and asked their questions in an order determined by lot. The priest transmitted the question, and as at Claros, the responses of the seeress were recorded by the priest, often translated into poetic form, and then delivered to the questioner.

These are the physical settings in which the oracles of the Classical world delivered their prophecies. In some of them, Nature had arranged an appropriate backdrop, while in others the setting was the result of art. Certainly these places were hallowed by association, but their similarities suggest that just as the towers built in so many cultures communicate pride and aspiration, the architecture of oracular sites was a physical manifestation of an archetypal oracular complex.

THE CAVERN, THE WELL, AND THE TREE

> *Thence (to Yggdrasil)*
> *. . . wise maidens three betake them—*
> *Under spreading boughs their bower stands—*
> *[Urdh one is hight, the other Versandi,*
> *Skuld the third: they scores did cut,]*
> *they laws did make, they lives did choose:*
> *for the children of men*
> *they marked their fates.*
>
> *Völuspá* 20

These are the words of the Völva, the ancient seeress from whom the Norse god Odin seeks wisdom. The journey, the holy tree, the sacred spring, the women who speak the words of fate—one or more of these appear wherever we find a seer. If these images are so pervasive, they must have an importance beyond creating a pleasant landscape. As oracles, we inhabit that larger world that transcends time and place. The unconscious speaks a symbolic language, so what does the symbolic setting we associate with an oracle mean?

Spontaneous prophecy strikes when and where it will, but moments of inspiration, while impressive, are more common in literature than in life. To be useful, an oracle must give answers when people have questions. One way to help the oracle to get answers and the questioner to understand them is to create a setting that will put both in the right state of mind.

Oracular rituals, like many other religious ceremonies, are more effective when they are also good theater. A well-produced drama helps actors and audience to believe in the characters, their problems, and their world until the play is done. To use some of the same techniques in a ritual does not lessen its validity. Whether the oracular setting is created physically or by evoking a mythic landscape, traditional imagery makes it easier for both the oracle and the questioner to transcend the barriers that ordinarily keep us from perceiving and interpreting the wisdom available to the unconscious.

The history of science includes numerous examples of moments in which the mind, pushed past the boundaries of reason, finds in a dream or a sudden shock the image that makes sense of the facts with which it has been struggling. The spiritual journeys of the seer may not be *real*, but if they lead to wisdom they can be *true*.

The Worldtree and the Norns

In the Germanic "map" of the cosmos, the worlds, or states of being, are arranged around Yggdrasil, the Worldtree, in much the same way as the sephiroth are arranged on the Tree of Life in the Kabbalah. Midgard, as its name implies, is somewhere in the middle. At the top of the Tree, we find Asgard, home of the gods, and far beneath it is Hel, where the ancestors dwell. The Tree has three roots, and beneath one of them lies Urðarbrunnr, the Well of Urð. This well is described in the passage quoted above, and in more detail in sections 15 and 16 of *Gylfaginning*, the first part of the Younger Edda.

Bauschatz defines the Old Norse *brun* as "the water source, some kind of enclosure that fixes it as a point in space, and the presence of an active process that results in the accumulation of water" (Bauschatz 1982, 17). Water that trickles from solid rock, or wells up from a muddy marsh in a clear stream, is clearly magical. When it contains minerals, there is a healing element as well. In addition to determining the lives of men, the Norns keep the Worldtree healthy by protecting its trunk with layers of white mud from the well. One is reminded of the waters of the Blue Lagoon in Iceland, saturated to opacity with minerals. Those who seek healing soak in its waters, and its mud is exported as a beauty aid. Springs are a source of purification. The waters of the Well of Urð are clearly a source of life as well. The Tree beneath whose root the Well lies is the Norse manifestation of the Worldtree, the *axis mundi* that is at once the sacred center, core, and support of all the worlds.

The verses from the *Völuspá* quoted above describe the three Norns, figures who are analogous to the three Fates of classical mythology. They are the archetypal originals, the embodiment of the oracular process. We hear of them first in *Völuspá* as three maidens who come from the land of the giants—they are, therefore, primal powers. In addition to tending the Worldtree, they manage the *ørlög* (an Old Norse term meaning the layers of destiny that events and choices have laid down in the Well) of the worlds.

"The Norns Weaving Destiny" by Arthur Rackham, 1911

This, however, is not an arbitrary process. Rather than making decisions about fate, they interact with it in a more organic fashion. The names of all three Norns are derived from forms of verbs meaning "to be." The first Norn, Urð, is concerned with what has been and has, therefore, already been laid down in the Well. The time, place, and family to which we are born are a part of our fate that cannot be changed. The name of the second Norn, Verðandi, is a present participle. She is the being and becoming of the ever-evolving present. She is the part of our ørlög that our choices constantly change. The name of the third Norn, Skuld, has to do with the future that is coming into being, the reality that, based on the present, *should* come to pass, the perpetually mutating probability.

In the lore, we are also told that there are other norns who operate on a smaller scale, tending the destinies of families and individuals, but the principles on which they operate are the same.

Spinners at the Sacred Spring

The Greek Moirae, who apportion out the lives of humankind, are associated with sacred water, although they may also be found in the Underworld, as when Plato describes them as sitting near the throne of Hades (*Republic* 617c). As we see in the "Orphic Hymn to the Fates" (LVIII) as translated by Thomas Taylor,

> *Daughters of darkling Nyx (Night), much named, draw near,*
> *infinite Moirai, and listen to my prayer;*
> *who in the heavenly lake, where waters white*
> *burst from a fountain hid in depths of night,*
> *and through a dark and stony cavern glide,*
> *a cave profound, invisible abide;*
> *from whence, wide coursing round the boundless earth,*
> *your power extends to those of mortal birth . . .*

Merlin's Cave

We find another legendary setting for a prophetic figure in the description of Merlin's cave that appears in Spenser's long poem *The Faerie Queen* (3:3–8):

> *There the wise Merlin whylome wont (they say)*
> *To make his wonne, low vnderneath the ground,*
> *In a deepe delue, farre from the vew of day,*
> *That of no liuing wight he mote be found,*
> *When so he counseld with his sprights enco[m]past round.*
> *And if thou euer happen that same way*

To trauell, goe to see that dreadfull place:
It is an hideous hollow caue (they say)
Vnder a rocke that lyes a little space
From the swift Barry, tombling downe apace,
Emongst the woodie hilles of Dyneuowre

Merlin's cave at Tintagel

As Howard Dobin observes, "This dark, underground space evokes all of the terror and temptation of trespassing on forbidden ground. . . . Merlin's cave in the *Faerie Queene* can be read as a topographical representation of the hazards of the prophetic enterprise" (Matthews 1999, 9). But it does so by invoking images we have already found elsewhere—the wilderness, the secret cave, and the stream.

The source of oracular wisdom is associated with water that wells up from deeper sources still. In his discussion of prophetic inspiration, Plutarch also emphasizes the role of the sacred spring:

. . . [T]he prophetic current and breath is most divine and holy, whether it issue by itself through the air or come in the company of running waters; for when it is instilled into the body, it creates in souls an unaccustomed and unusual temperament, the peculiarity of which it is hard to describe with exactness, but analogy offers many comparisons. It is likely that by warmth and diffusion it opens up certain passages through which impressions of the future are transmitted . . . (*De Defectu Oraculae* 40)

We see in these descriptions several elements that we will encounter again and again as we explore the lore of the seer. But to find the sacred well and the holy tree requires a journey.

THE ORACULAR ENVIRONMENT

In the summer of 2001, I had the opportunity to experience oracular trance in a real-world context that included all of this imagery. I went to Britain to conduct an oracle workshop with Caitlin Matthews, an old friend and an inspiring teacher of esoteric Celtic lore. She had made arrangements for our group to meet at Rosemerryn Wood in Cornwall, near Penzance, a house that was then being used as a conference center (now a bed-and-breakfast—guests are invited to explore). It was located just down the road from a stone circle called the Merry Maidens, which I had visited when I was doing research for a novel about Tristan and Iseult called *The White Raven*, and which I had identified as being on one of the major British ley lines.

As we drew near, I was amused to notice that every time the road dipped into a crease between the rolling hills, the hedgerows to either side arched overhead, so that we were driving through a tunnel of trees. But not until Caitlin led me into the overgrown garden behind the house did I understand why she had been smiling so mysteriously.

Upon a mound grew a holly tree from whose branches fluttered votive ribbons. Below it, a pathway slanted steeply down into the hill. Peering into its shadowed depths, I made out the gleam of water.

"Hmm. Guess I better revise the path working," I told Caitlin. "All the images we need are already here."

What I was looking at was the Boleigh Fogou, a stone-lined subterranean chamber. It is one of a number of such sites in Cornwall and northern

Scotland, built during the Celtic Iron Age for purposes unknown. Although they are constructed in the same way as passage graves, no human remains have ever been found in them. The water inside was the result of seeping groundwater, not a well, but that was not apparent to the eye. One of the stones at the entry in front of a little side chamber was incised with the outline of a warrior, clearly the guardian.

The side chamber at the Boleigh Fogou

On the last evening of the workshop, we went out to the fogou and set tealights at intervals down the slope, so that the passage seemed framed by stars. One by one, each of us descended and took her seat upon the chair we had set within. The words with which we had practiced were said, the songs were sung, and each of us in turn went into trance with a question and reported what she saw.

What was interesting was that each of us seemed to arrive at a different level of consciousness, some contacting primal energies, while for

THE WAY OF THE ORACLE

others the answers were more personal. My own question was about the purpose of the fogou, and my vision suggested that during the Celtic period, at least, it had been used for religious purposes. I saw the fortified settlement that had guarded the chamber and the seekers who had kept vigil there. The ley line that passes through the Merry Maidens can be contacted through the stones of the circle, but during the great festivals, sitting in the fogou, which lies underground, would be like sitting in the middle of a flowing stream of power. This was not one of the holy days, but I could sense some of that energy and was both sorry and relieved that my allotted time in the chamber was too short for it to carry me away.

Although I do not believe that the fogou was intended as an oracular chamber, all the imagery I had previously identified as conducive to vision was certainly there, and that evening still ranks as one of my most memorable experiences with oracle work.

The Archetypal Setting

What, then, are the characteristic elements of the oracular setting? First, the surrounding landscape must be Otherworldly, or at least awe-inspiring and difficult to access. When we approach, we should expect to find one or more sacred trees. Although we may have to climb to reach the sacred site, the approach should also involve a passage beneath the earth, through a tunnel or into a cavern. At the site, we should expect to find a well or spring. Although it is not mentioned in the sources, we will also need some source of light, provided by a lamp, torch, or fire.

This is the secret, twilight path that leads to the Well of Memory, "the well-head where the pale white cypress grows," says Dion Fortune's song (1956, 166). The journey is itself a powerful metaphor. Images of descent suggest relaxation and a shift in consciousness, as when we speak of sinking into trance or falling asleep. The dead lie beneath the earth, and so it is not surprising that one popular place to search for their wisdom is the Underworld. In the poems called *The Speaking of the Völva, The Shorter Seeress' Prophecy*, and *The Dream of Baldr* the god Odin journeys to Hella's realm in the depths beneath the Worldtree in order to consult the Völva, the archetypal seeress who speaks the lines with which this chapter began. In the Prose Edda we learn how Hermod journeyed to Hel in an attempt to retrieve Baldr. A more detailed account of that journey is given in the *History of the Danes* by Saxo Grammaticus (I:31), when Hading travels to the Underworld. Odysseus and Aeneas journey to Hades to consult the spirits of their fathers. As we shall see, a number of oracular sites in the ancient world required seers and questioners to physically descend to reach the oracular chamber.

However, ascent to a place from which one can see out over the earth or talk to the gods is also a powerful metaphor for the transcendence that brings vision. When Odin wishes to see what is happening on the earth, he ascends to Hlithskjalf, his Seat of Seeing. Although oracles are not shamans, shamans often perform as oracles, so it is worth mentioning the many examples of directional imagery in the shamanic literature. Mircea Eliade identifies a basic layout of three cosmic zones, sky, earth, and underworld (which may be subdivided), linked by an axis in the form of a mountain, pillar, or tree, up and down which the shaman travels to speak to the spirits. The mountain and Worldtree are also symbols of the sacred center, represented in Classical oracular chambers by the omphalos stone.

As Eliade points out,

> this cosmological concept does not belong exclusively to the ideology of Siberian and Central Asian shamanism, nor, in fact, of any other shamanism. It is a universally disseminated idea connected with the belief in the possibility of direct communication with the sky. (Eliade 1964, 264)

The shaman journeys for many purposes—to learn if a sacrifice has been accepted and to receive predictions concerning the weather and the coming harvest, or in other words, to answer the same kinds of questions put to oracles in other lands.

Creating the Context

In the *Saga of Erik the Red* 4, we see an example of how a temporary setting for an oracle was made:

> Thorkel invited the seeress to visit and preparations were made to entertain her well, as was the custom of the time when a woman of this type was received. A high seat was set for her, complete with cushion. This was to be stuffed with chicken feathers. . . . A

porridge of kid's milk was made for her and as meat she was given the hearts of all the animals available there. . . . Once the tables had been cleared away, Thorkel approached Thorbjorg and asked . . . how soon he could expect an answer to what he had asked and everyone wished to know. She answered that she would not reveal this until the next day after having spent the night there. Late the following day she was provided with things she required to carry out her magic rites. . . . She asked for women who knew the chants required for carrying out magic rites, which are called ward songs *(varðlokkur)*. . . . The women formed a warding ring around the platform raised for sorcery, with Thorbjorg perched atop it. . . . After that people approached the wise woman to learn what each of them was most curious to know. She made them good answer, and little that she predicted did not occur.

The great oracles of the past are silent, their treasures scattered, their foundations reduced to archaeological sites over which tourists crawl. The spontaneous psychic needs no setting; however, the elaborate establishments of the ancient oracles were intended not only to inspire the seers, but also to open the minds of the questioners. There are times when even the gods can only offer good advice, and in ordinary circumstances, the human mind puts up defenses against it.

Although most of us will never have the opportunity to work in a dedicated location, we can see from the description of the oracular rite in Viking Age Greenland that a temporary setting can be created with minimal props and invested with power through imagery. In reconstructing oracular practice, I have adopted a dual strategy in which the physical layout is supported by a guided meditation. The more we create externally, the less work the imagination will need to do; however, the essential tool for any spiritual practice is the mind, and a trained seer can do the work without any props at all.

When I began this work, my goal was to serve the community. Following the Scandinavian model, in which the seers journeyed from one farmstead to another to conduct sessions, I go where the people can be gathered. Most of the time this is a living room, rented space in the local Unitarian Church, or a hotel function room. But some of the settings, such as the Cornish fogou described earlier, have been more memorable.

One of my most inspiring memories is of a session during the thirty-year anniversary festival of the Society for Creative Anachronism. Having passed from the medieval encampment to the Norse enclave and from there to a leafy hillside outside the festival boundaries, I was already detached from ordinary reality. By the time I sat down on a stool on a cowhide, guarded by warriors who wore spangenhelms and leaned on spears, the path working to move me into the Nordic sector of the collective unconscious was no longer necessary.

The most impressive chair in which I ever sat was a huge, carved affair that looked as if it had been built for a giant; it had been found in some Mexican antique store and provided by the organizers of an ADF conference in Tucson. The most powerful outdoor setting in which I have worked was the grassy slope of a sinkhole in the area between the walls of the rift at Thingvellir in Iceland, where the energies of the natural forces were so strong that it was difficult to get a fix on human needs.

Diana Paxson and Lorrie Wood with the Great Chair at the ADF festival

FARING TO THE OTHERWORLD

The other way to reach the place of prophecy is through a guided meditation or path working in which the journey is narrated or visualized.

THE WAY OF THE ORACLE

The more mundane your physical surroundings, the more important this inner journey will be. Although we have no accounts of such a journey in the context of an oracular session, spirit journeying is listed as one of Odin's skills in the Norse *Heimskringla*. The ways in which this skill can be used to seek answers will be discussed in Chapter III.

In some oracle groups, only the seer makes this journey, either directed by a guide who speaks to him or her alone, or in silence, while the rest of the group waits or sings. For example, note how Rod Landreth uses imagery in order to move into oracular trance:

> I breathe and sort of tell myself . . . ok go into Trance. Since most of the time I have to really make an effort to hold back this state . . . I just sort of "fall" into at first a light trance. Once I'm in that state, I direct myself through set imagery (go through a glade to Yggdrasil, then around the base till I see Wyrd's Well), and then, through a mnemonic device of plunging my hands into the waters of the Well, I pull up what I can only call a Skein between my hands. From this point, I am ready to see/look into the probabilities for the answer(s) the querent asks for.

My own preference is to include the rest of the group in the path working because I believe that this increases the rapport between the seer and the questioners. It also supports belief and makes the ritual more interesting. The more deeply the questioner is drawn into the experience, the more likely he is to pay attention. You will find exercises for developing such a path working in Part Two.

III

THE PROPHETIC PROCESS: TECHNIQUES FOR ACHIEVING ORACULAR TRANCE

Twenty women of all ages and origins are gathered at a YMCA camp in Northern California's coastal mountains. For the Goddess Festival, the cabin has been hung with goddess banners and retitled Themis Lodge. I'm scheduled to talk about oracle work and give a demonstration, but I don't have my usual support team. How can I give them a sense of what this process is like without the dog-and-pony show I usually put on? I've had twenty years of practice, but can I do this alone?

This is a good group of people. Some have a fair amount of experience, but I'm putting the demonstration first, so if anyone needs help after the trance work, I can deal with that during the lecture. I ask one woman to be a timekeeper and another to act as watcher, and I explain what we're going to do. This has to be a bare-bones version of the process, so I need to focus on essentials—purification, invoking the Powers we're working with, binding the group together, and getting myself to a place where I can find answers.

I sprinkle everyone with water "from the sacred spring." We sing together, and I sit down on a chair that has been transformed into the seat of the seeress by being covered with a shawl. I take up my drum to accompany our journey to the Oracle Cave. This path is not so well worn as the road to the Norse underworld, but it's more accessible to people from mixed traditions. Soon, inner vision shows me torchlight gleaming on the sacred pool. I remind the others to stay outside, start singing the passage song, and move within.

As the group takes over the singing, I feel my awareness change. Open, passive, I pull the veil over my face to signal I'm ready. Energy flows like the water that bubbles from the depths of the well. With each question, I look into the water, and images and answers come. But all too soon another voice tells us

that the "hour grows late." It takes all my discipline to detach, turn my awareness away from the cave, resume control of my body, and take up the drum to
narrate our journey back to ordinary reality. Another song helps us all to fit
back into our bodies. I thank the Norns and the ancestors, open the circle, and
offer salt to anyone who needs help to ground and center.

Now that they've seen a sample of oracle work, the group is ready to learn
more, and I know that shifting to left-brain thinking for another hour will get
us all back to normal by dinnertime. Later, some of the women will thank me
for answering their questions, or confess how much they wanted to go into the
cave with me, or comment that the journey put them into the deepest trance
state they've ever known.

As for me, I'm glad I was able to get the job done.

IMPROMPTU ORACLES

In its simplest form, the oracular process consists of a question and an
answer. The medieval chronicler Giraldus Cambrensus reported on this
kind of encounter in his description of Irish seers:

> When you consult them about some problem, they immediately
> go into a trance and lose control of their senses, as if they are pos-
> sessed. They do not answer the question put to them in any logical
> way. Words stream from their mouths, incoherently and appar-
> ently meaningless and without any sense at all, but all the same
> well expressed; and if you listen carefully to what they say you will
> receive the solution to your problem. When it is all over, they will
> recover from their trance, as if they were ordinary people waking
> from a heavy sleep, but you have to give them a good shake before
> they regain control of themselves. . . . They seem to receive this gift
> of divination through visions which they see in their dreams. (In
> Matthews 1999, 14)

This sounds like Fedelm's prophecy in the *Tain*, although I doubt that
Maeve had to shake the *ban-drui* to get her back to normal. In the Celtic
lore, the question itself is sufficient to invoke oracular trance in a seer
who is by training or natural talent conditioned to respond to such a cue.
At times, although a human need starts the process, other factors, such
as a deity's need to communicate, determine the outcome.

ORACLE RITES

In some cultures, oracles are not only impromptu and informal, but some-times involuntary, while in others they are given only in a highly struc-tured ceremony. Spontaneous answers generally come from those with overwhelming natural talent or an intensive training, like the Druids. To analyze the oracular *process*, we must look at the more formal ceremonial traditions. The Neoplatonic philosopher Iamblichus, who is one of the more dependable sources of information on Classical magical practices, clearly sets the oracular process within the context of ritual:

> These things, therefore, are plain to view, namely: the abundance of offerings, the established law of the whole sacred Observance, and such other things as are performed in a manner worthy of a god, prior to the oracular responding, such as the baths of the prophet-ess, her fasting for three entire days, her abiding in the interior shrine and having there already the light and enjoying it a long time. (*On the Oracle at Didyma* 3, 7)

In the previous chapter, we saw that there are certain images that recur in oracular settings. What does the ancient literature tell us about the rituals that took place there?

Preparation

In the Mediterranean, both questioners and seers were carefully pre-pared for the experience. Already influenced by the rugged splendor of the gorge at Delphi or by the majestic Sacred Way that led from the shore to the great oracular temple of Didyma, questioners would prepare for the ceremony through purification and by making offerings. At this time, singers, such as the choirs who accompanied petitioners to Claros, would offer their songs to the god. The seers also underwent a preparatory process. At Claros, Didyma, and Delphi, they were sequestered before the ritual, abstaining from sexual relations. They fasted anywhere from twenty-four hours to three days. According to Plutarch, at Delphi,

> they guard the chastity of the priestess, and keep her life free from all association and contact with strangers, and take the omens before the oracle, thinking that it is clear to the god when she has the temperament and disposition suitable to submit to the inspiration

without harm to herself. The power of the spirit does not affect all persons nor the same persons always in the same way, but it only supplies an enkindling and an inception, as has been said, for them that are in a proper state to be affected and to undergo the change. (*De Defectu Oraculae* 51)

A ritual bath would cleanse the spirit as well as the body. Donning special garments distinguished the ordinary human persona from that of the seer. Sequestration separated the ordinary human world from the sanctuary of the oracle. At Delphi, omens provided additional insurance. The goat selected for the offering to the god was sprinkled with water. Its trembling signified that it had accepted its fate and the sacrifice, and the oracular ritual could go forward. If, on the other hand, the goat did not shiver, the rite was called off.

In the story of the Greenland völva, the seeress, instead of withdrawing, prepares by immersing herself in the environment in which she will be seeking answers:

> Thorkell bid the spakona to his dwelling and a good reception was made for her as was usual when this sort of a woman was received. . . . Thorkell the farmer took the wise-woman by the hand and led her to the seat which had been prepared for her. He asked her to cast her eyes over his home, household and hearth-fires . . . she was given a gruel made from goat's milk, and had the main dish of hearts from the various kinds of animals that were available there. . . . When the tables had been removed Thorkell went over to Thorbjorg and asked her how she liked his home and people's behavior there, and how soon she would know the answer to his question which everyone wanted to learn. She replied that she would not give any answer until the following morning, when she slept there overnight first. (*Saga of Erik the Red* 4)

I believe that by sleeping at the farmstead and eating the food grown there, the völva established a physical and psychic connection with the local energies that helped her to answer questions about the land and the people living there. One Irish seer told his successor "that whenever he could not decide on some dark-meaning question which the men of Ireland posed him he should consume some of its fruit, corn, fish, milk or chestnuts" (Minahane, in Matthews 1999, 11).

Matthews goes on to suggest that those born outside northwestern Europe may find it hard to draw on the ancestral blood links: "They should forge new relationships with the lands in which they now live. This creates a different dynamic, for the music of the native tradition is being played on an instrument that is tuned to a different cultural continuum. The success of the transfer of a diasporic tradition depends largely on the maturity and adaptability of the transplanted individual" (Matthews 1999, 15).

Drinking water from the sacred spring might also be a way to connect to the local energy. According to Iamblichus,

> [i]t is acknowledged by everybody that the oracle at Kolophon gives its responses through the medium of water. There is a spring in a house underground, and from this the prophet drinks. On certain appointed nights, many sacred ceremonies having taken place beforehand, he drinks, and delivers oracles, but he is not seen by the beholders who are present. It is manifest from this, therefore, that that water possesses an oracular quality. (*Theurgia* III, 7)

Transition: Cues and Conditioning

However short or long the preparations, at last there comes the moment that everyone has been waiting for, when the oracle moves from normal to nonordinary consciousness, the trance state in which she is able to access information and answer questions. We have no first person narratives in which ancient seers recorded their experiences, but we do have descriptions of what went on in the oracle chambers, including how the seers signaled the unconscious that it was time to shift gears and actually made the transition from one state to the next.

The High Seat

Just as the Greenland völva spoke from a specially constructed *seidhjallr*, which was an elevated seat or platform, at Claros, Delphi, and at Didyma, the oracle was seated on a special seat. This was apparently an important cue. The act of sitting on an elevated seat, like that of descending into an oracular chamber, is a physical analogue for shifting into a different state of consciousness. In Didyma, the seeress sat upon an "axon," which must have been some kind of column. At Branchidae, she sat on a wheel (also presumably supported by some kind of block or column). At Delphi, she was perched on the famous tripod, a three-legged stand normally used to hold something like a cauldron. Tripods were prized as gifts. They were not, however, usually utilized as seating. The one pictured at Delphi supports a shallow bowl in which the pythia sits.

A bronze tripod, National Museum at Athens

To sit on any of these must have required good balance, and to remain upright while in a state of mantic enthusiasm might be taken as proof that the seeress was really in trance. In another passage, however, Iamblichus mentions the seeress "sitting in the inner shrine, upon the bronze chair with three feet or upon the four-footed chair sacred to the divinities" (*Theurgia* III, 7), so apparently the tripod was not the only seat from which prophecy might be given.

In Viking Age Scandinavia, a *seidhjallr* is often mentioned when a spae working is described. Such constructions were used not only for spae, but for other kinds of sorcery as well. The one in the *Saga of Erik the Red* had a special cushion of hen's feathers; it was probably a temporary construction, wood in Greenland being hard to come by. However, amulets in the form of a chair carved from a log, which may represent the seidhjallr, have been found in the graves of völvas (Price 2002, 164–68).

Viking "gobstol" chair

Seidhjallr's high seat

IN SEARCH OF THE ORACLE

An even earlier Germanic example also indicates a connection between elevation and prophecy. The Roman historian Tacitus reports that the Bructeri seeress Veleda was asked to arbitrate a conflict between the Roman citizens of what is now Cologne and the Tencteri tribe: "In order to inspire (the ambassadors) with respect they were prevented from seeing her. She dwelt in a lofty tower, and one of her relatives, chosen for the purpose, conveyed, like the messenger of a divinity, the questions and answers" (*Histories* 4, 65). Tacitus may have been using Classical models to interpret the stories he heard—the procedure sounds a lot like that of the Delphic oracle. Lindsay Davis has suggested that Veleda took up residence in an old Roman signal tower, but I think that what Tacitus interpreted as a tower may have been some kind of elevated seat or platform similar to the seidhjallr of the later Viking Age.

High seats set up for a seidh rite

THE WAY OF THE ORACLE

Apparently the act of sitting down in a special place was itself a powerful cue for shifting consciousness. In my own experience this has certainly been true. Although I have done oracular work sitting in ordinary chairs, when I climb into an elevated seat, such as the tall chair that was built for our seidh group many years ago, I feel a physical sense of release from ordinary consciousness. In fact, the sense of detachment is strong enough that I rest my staff on the floor in front of me and use it as a grounding line.

These days, other groups that do spaework have also constructed their own permanent seidhjallrs in the form of elevated chairs whose pieces come apart for travel.

Stocks and Staves

Anyone who has seen *The Lord of the Rings* film trilogy is familiar with the wizard's staff. A wooden staff or stick is often part of the oracle's regalia. The seeress at Branchidae held a stave. The pythia of Delphi is portrayed holding a sprig of laurel in memory of the rod Apollo is said to have given to the legendary founder.

Viking Age wrought-iron seidh-staff

A staff was a defining accoutrement of a Norse völva and may provide her title—"staff-bearer," from the Old Norse *völr*, "rod." Descriptions of Norse magic include references to the *gand*, probably a wand; the *gambann*-twig, probably used in operant magic; and the larger *stafr* or *seidhstafr*, the staff the Greenland völva used: "In her hand she carried a staff with a knob on it. It was decorated with brass and set with stones under the knob" (*Saga of Erik the Red* 4). In the *Laxdaela Saga* 76, a grave is identified as that of a völva because it includes "a great sorcery-staff *[seidhstafr]*." In *The Viking Way*, Neil Price identifies cane-length wooden and wrought-iron rods (some adorned with images) found in the graves of priestesses as possible seidh-staffs (2002, 181–204). Amulets in the form of metal rings with charms, possibly representing staffs, have also been found.

Diana Paxson at Thingvellir, with staff

In the form of seidh reconstructed by Annette Høst of the Scandinavian Center for Shamanic Studies, students go to the woods to find a staff, which they "ride" while journeying. She says:

> When the people I have worked with have chosen or cut their staffs, their guidance have [sic] been this scanty information plus spirit instruction or intuition. It is peculiar how the very most of the staffs turn out being of the same length. And off they go on the journey, holding onto their staffs. What do they tell upon returning? That the staff is a power antenna, it is a lightning rod, it grows hot, it comes alive and vibrates, it moves like a snake in the hands, it keeps the focus and direction of flight clear, at the same time as it grounds. It is the tree of life, connecting the lower world and the sky world, power flowing through it. (*www.shamanism.dk/Artikel—THE STAFF AND THE SONG.htm*)

Most of the seers in my own group have staffs. Those of us who travel to festivals in other parts of the country make ours from paint-extender rods that can be taken apart and packed in a suitcase. Three packs will give you a top, a bottom, and three middle pieces. We add a brass knob to the top and sand and carve the sections with symbols or images, sometimes set with stones.

Spirit Songs

At the Classical oracles, the ritual process included offering hymns of praise to the god. It is not clear if this occurred as part of the actual questioning, or whether these songs could be heard by the seer or were performed earlier in the sequence. It is certain, however, that song was an essential part of the process in Scandinavia. In the story of the Greenland völva, after all the preparations have been made and the völva is seated on the seidhjallr, the participants encounter an obstacle. No one seems to know the traditional song known as the *varðlokkur*. After some argument, they persuade a young woman called Gudrid to sing.

> The women made a ring around Thorbjorg, who was seated up on the seidhjallr. Gudrid sang the song so beautifully and well that they were sure they had never heard lovelier singing. The spákona

thanked her for the song, and said that many spirits had come to that place, "which before had been turned from us and would grant us no obedience, as what had been sung seemed beautiful for them to hear. And now many things are revealed to me which were before hidden from me and others." (*Saga of Erik the Red* 4)

In this passage, the song is being sung to summon the spirits, but I think it likely that it had an effect on the seeress as well. Certainly this seems to be the case in shamanic practice. An Eskimo shaman called Aua described how he called his spirits with a simple, repetitious song "until he bursts into tears; then he feels a boundless joy" (Eliade 1964, 91). Whatever effect such singing has on a spirit, it certainly is autohypnotic. Possession of such songs, given by the spirits, is common in the shamanic literature, and singing them is generally a part of the process by which the shaman enters trance.

Shamanic singing is a major part of seidh practice as taught by Annette Høst, who says:

It is said that the seidrsong was ecstatic song. To me ecstasy means a state where you have let go so much of ego, control, and convention that the power of the universe flushes through you unhindered. And that is the first trait of shamanic singing: that you sing from a source that is bigger than yourself, and let power flow through you as song. In other words, the song is sung in an altered state of awareness, or in trance. And when we start to sing like that, we can experience a marvelous shift in our voice, our breathing and endurance, the power and effect of our utterance. The song sings us.

There is a second trait of the ecstatic song that makes it shamanic: the song has a definite purpose. We sing open the doors to the otherworld. We sing out to our spirit helpers, so they may know we're calling them. We sing to a tree to honour its beautiful power. We sing the invisible threads between us and our spirit helpers stronger. We sing a mound open, so we can talk with our ancestors. We sing pains and spirits of illness away. We sing thanks to the plants we harvest.

This gets us to the third trait. Shamanic songs or chants are not composed or constructed. They are found, heard, gotten, when we are inspired. They arrive, arise, unfold. And then they burst from me, when I am full, full, and cannot contain them any longer. The songs visit us. Sometimes they stay with us for a long time, sometimes they leave again fast. Sometimes they have words, sometimes just sounds. (*www.shamanism.dk/Artikel—THE STAFF AND THE SONG.htm*)

In her ceremonies, a group of women gather around the seeress and begin free-form singing, or toning, as the spirit moves them, which successfully carries the seeress into a state in which she can ride the energy and journey to find answers.

The völva in the *Saga of Erik the Red* clearly needs a very specific song in order to reach a state in which she can perceive the spirits. We have no recordings of the *varðlokkur* to experiment with, but the shamanic literature suggests that what matters is the fact that the seer has been conditioned to respond to the song. For use in my own group, I adapted the tune from "Stolt øli," an old Norwegian folksong, and gave it new words.

> *Seeress (or "Seer now"), thy way*
> *through the worlds thou must win,*
> *Farther and faster, and deeper within,*
> *Fare onward, ever onward, ever on.*

That song has become a dependable cue that we can use to pass through the gate to the Underworld. Different songs help us to move to other locations, such as the Well of Wyrd or the Oracle Cave. By conditioning ourselves to respond to a specific piece of music, we can fine-tune our ability to reach very specific places in the inner landscape or contact specific spiritual beings.

Entheogens and Enthousiasmos

Since ancient times, scholars have debated whether the prophetic *enthousiasmos* was induced by some physical means, such as the vapors that are said to have flowed from the depths at Delphi. More recently, Steven Leto published an article averring that the Viking Age seeresses achieved trance with the aid of *Amanita muscaria* or psilocybin (Leto 2000, 64). For an excellent discussion of the arguments for and against the use of entheogens in modern shamanism, see Chapter 4 of Jenny Blain's *Nine Worlds of Seid-Magic*.

Amanita muscaria, hemp, ergot, psilocybin, and henbane are mentioned as having been used in magical contexts in other parts of Europe and Asia. Given that spirit-workers in many cultures *do* use entheogens to support, extend, and empower their work, we need to at least consider the arguments for their use in European oracular practice.

MAGIC MUSHROOMS

Since the 1960s, theories about the use of psychedelic mushrooms in Norse magic have proliferated. *Amanita muscaria* is said to have induced the berserker rage and was used by Saami shamans to achieve visionary trance. However, *Amanita* is not found in Iceland, from which most of our information on seidh comes. The other candidate for such use is *Psilocybin semilanceata,* which does grow in Iceland as well as all over Europe and Scandinavia. Steven Leto explored the possibility that they were used in seidh magic in an interesting article in *Shaman's Drum.* His research on the effects indicated that

> both *A. muscaria* and the *Psilocybes* seem to be capable of catalyzing ecstatic experiences, with feelings of unity and bliss, but the content and quality of the experiences may be significantly different. A prevalence of literary motifs and themes involving intense salivation, significant changes in muscular-motor control, dramatic size distortions in visual perception, and a tendency to fall asleep and have lucid dream-vision states may hint at *A. muscaria* usage. In contrast, motifs of strong visual distortions and web-like hallucinations, accompanied by pronounced experiences of intuition and precognition, might be indicative of *Psilocybe* mushrooms. (Leto 2000, 60)

Leto's efforts to identify mushroom references and symbolism in the eddas and sagas unfortunately rest on translations of the material that are not supported by the interpretations of other scholars. This does not necessarily mean that mushrooms were never used in Norse magic. In a psilocybin experience, yawning is common at one point, and at the beginning of the seidh trance in *Hrolf Kraki's Saga,* we are told that the seeress yawns. In general, however, the effects produced by psilocybin and other psychedelics seem more consistent with the kind of visionary work known as "going under the cloak" to meditate on a problem than with the kind of controlled performance described in the accounts of oracular seidh.

THE FAMOUS FUMES OF DELPHI

Was the pythia at Delphi put into trance by breathing some kind of narcotic fumes? Plutarch tells us,

> I think, then, that the exhalation is not in the same state all the time, but that it has recurrent periods of weakness and strength. Of the proof on which I depend I have as witnesses many foreigners and all the officials and servants at the shrine. It is a fact that the room in which they seat those who would consult the god is filled, not frequently or with any regularity, but as it may chance from time to time, with a delightful fragrance coming on a current of air which bears it towards the worshippers. (*De Defectu Oraculae* 51)

For centuries this "efflorescence" was held to explain the oracle's power; however, when the French excavated the site in the 1890s, no trace of narcotic gas was found. The actual site of the adyton, the oracular chamber, was not found until the 1920s, and although the archaeologists reported small fissures, there were no gaping chasms. But nothing in the world of science is so certain as that hypotheses exist to be challenged. In 1979, geologist Jelle de Boer noticed a fault line running beneath the Delphic sanctuary. In 1995, he met archaeologist John Hale, and a remarkable partnership, described with all the suspense of a detective story by William J. Broad in *Oracle* (2006), began. They demonstrated a strong probability that at one time the fissures could have emitted ethylene gas, used during the 1920s as an anesthetic.

Broad reports that medical researcher Henry Spillar tested the effects of ethylene gas by administering it to a local housewife. Eventually the doctor and the woman's husband joined her. "[T]he three of them started giggling and laughing and slapping their legs, sitting in their makeshift *adyton,* rocking on their lawn chairs, switching positions, jabbering happily, oblivious of most everything but their own bliss" (Broad 2007, 25). Clearly, although the physiological effects of the gas were enough to produce an altered state, that state would not result in prophecy in a subject who had not been prepared and conditioned to expect it or who didn't have the support of a ritual.

To quote Plutarch once more:

> Whenever, then, the imaginative and prophetic faculty is in a state of proper adjustment for attempering itself to the spirit as to a drug, inspiration in those who foretell the future is bound to come; and whenever the conditions are not thus, it is bound not to come, or when it does come to be misleading, abnormal, and confusing, as we know in the case of the priestess who died not so long ago. (*De Defectu Oraculae* 51)

The latter comment refers to the priestess who died after being forced to prophesy when the omens were not right, a story discussed in more detail in Chapter VII.

A further consideration is the fact that the ethylene vapors, if that's what they were, flowed intermittently. The other Mediterranean oracles produced good answers for their clients without intoxicating vapors or potions. Clearly, though an entheogen might make the trance work easier, it is not the *source* of the visions.

The Medium and the Message

As we have seen, an oracular state could have been triggered by a variety of stimuli, from undergoing a sequence of purifications to entering a setting dedicated to that purpose, ingesting water or drugs, or having contact with symbolic items. The fact that there are "born seers" who can enter a prophetic state without any preparation whatsoever shows that the ability to do so lies within the natural spectrum of human talents, but the oracles of the Classical world were not dependent on the availability of natural seers. Oracular rituals and practices must have enabled an individual to achieve a receptive state on cue. Once that state was achieved, those in need of information could put their questions. But where did, and do, the seers find their replies?

For the *ban-drui* Fedelm, the information seems to have appeared as soon as she "looked." In the *Saga of Erik the Red*, Gudrid's song attracted many spirits. Dronke interprets the word "spáganda" in *Völuspá* 29 as "spirits of prophecy" and makes a case for an archetypal or spirit völva as the source of information for the seeress who is speaking to Odin.

In the twelfth-century "Song of the Sun," the speaker sits "on the chair of the nornir" for nine days and then is "raised up" on a horse to see visions of the Otherworld (Price 2002, 208). This could refer to a spirit journey while sitting on the seidhjallr. In *Føstbraedhrasaga* 9, the völva says that she has "caused *gandir* [spirits, possibly in wolf form] to run far in the night, and I have now become wise about those things that I did not know before."

When working in the Norse tradition, my own method has been to use a visualized journey to move my awareness to the gate of the Norse Underworld, where the god Odin went to consult the archetypal Völva, and ride the song to which I'm trained to respond through the gate into a much deeper, completely passive state in which hearing a question stimulates a vision. If nothing happens, I call upon the raven who is my spirit helper to lead me to an answer. Some questions require me to journey to different places in the Otherworld, usually to speak to deities.

For the oracle priests and priestesses of the Mediterranean world, the source of all wisdom was the god or spirit associated with the oracular site, such as Dione, Zeus, Hera, and Gaia. By the late Classical period, this deity was almost universally Apollo. The oracles of Apollo are recorded as being spoken in the first person, from the perspective of the god. But nowhere is it indicated that the priest or priestess takes on the aspect of the god himself. This is apparently not the kind of full-body possession we find in Afro-diasporic traditions such as voodoo. The kind of trance involved would seem to be similar to modern "channeling," in which a medium in trance speaks the words transmitted to him or her by a higher power, such as an angel or ascended master, and the words are then written down by someone not in trance, rather in the way the responses of the pythia were recorded by the attending priests at Delphi.

Although most of my practice has been in the Northern tradition, with my husband I have worked in the Hellenic tradition as well. Interestingly enough, when I served as priestess in an oracular session in a Greek style, I found myself speaking Apollo's words in answer to the questions while simultaneously aware of the god's independent presence. This was neither the passive state in which I receive simple imagery and information nor the very active experience of possession, in which the deity takes over the mind and body. Instead, it seems to be quite close to the kind of consciousness involved in channeling. My experience has been that answers can also come directly, from spirits or from gods.

Clearing the Channels

Those who do oracle work today describe their process in a variety of ways. Cues such as drumming, a song, or deep, regular breathing work well for many and are often accompanied by visualization.

> When working with Seiðhjallr, we use a combination of conditioned breath, sound, visual, and tactile cues. In a pinch, to the sufficiently trained practitioner, these cues can be internalized. When something comes to me spontaneously, it is often as a compulsion that arises with no clear source ("take this bridge instead of that one!"). If circumstances warrant . . . I will run through my breathing cues to still myself and listen better—or, alternately, to close down the errant non-ordinary input, as it's not always useful.
>
> Lorrie Wood

> A full-blown ceremony, with either a large or a small group, provides the setting, songs, drumming, guide, etc., to produce the trance. When working alone, during my first years, I used a tape or CD of shamanic drumming, which can be very helpful both for moving into and moving out of trance. Now I often drum for myself—I've gotten pretty good at automatic drumming, and I like it. Other times I just use very simple meditation techniques. Sometimes I use some hypnotic sound in the environment: the sound of wind in the trees, a blizzard of hissing snow, the intense buzzing of cicadas or crickets, the trilling of a backyard full of toads during a spring rain, sometimes even the drone of airplane engines during an airplane flight. These are actually some of my favorites, especially the toads and the crickets!
>
> Winifred Hodge Rose

Facilitating the Process

Although we have a great deal of information about the preparations and results of the Delphic oracular ritual, we have no script for the actual questioning. However, scholars in Scandinavian Studies such as Bertha

Philpotts and Terry Gunnell have speculated that the poems in dialogue form in the Elder Edda may have been modeled on pagan ritual dramas. In the three poems in which the god Odin consults a völva, I believe that we find a format that might have been used for oracular seidh.

In *The Dream of Baldr* 7 and 8, Odin rides to the eastern gate of Hel and chants spells to summon the Völva from her grave mound and learn why his son Baldr has been having death dreams. She ends each answer with the words, *"nauðug sagðak, nú mun ek thegja,"* "from need I spoke, now must I be silent." His response is, "Be not silent, Völva! Thou wilt I question 'til everything I want I know!"

The repeated phrasing suggests a ritual pattern. We also find such a pattern in *Völuspá (The Spae of the Völva),* in which the völva is apparently in a more cooperative mood. In lines 28 through 36, we are told that she was "sitting out," perhaps on, if not in, a grave mound, when Odin "her eye did seek" and gave her rings and a necklace to hear her spell speaking and spell magic. She signals the end of many of her answers with the phrase, *"Vituð ér enn—eða hvat?"* "Would you know more, or what?" (*Völuspá* 30).

In the *Shorter Spae of the Völva* 4, the seeress ends her answers with a similar line: "Much have I said to thee, and will (say) more, what you need to know, Would you have more?"

When I first began to search the eddas for clues regarding how a spae session might have been managed, the similarities between these three poems reminded me strongly of the cues given in trance work. Although none of the saga accounts feature this kind of dialogue, it seemed to me that such a pattern could have been based on ritual practice, and we have found that ritual phrases do indeed work as a powerful cue for the seer to seek visions and signal readiness for another question.

Recovery

How the process of question and answer was handled in the Mediterranean oracles varied from time to time and place to place. Sometimes the querents asked their questions directly and were answered directly by the seer. But this was not always so. At Colophon, the seer received only the numbers of the questions and the names of the questioners. At other times, the answers were processed into verse by a thespode. In other traditions, querents did communicate directly with the seer.

Whatever the process, the final element in the oracular process is recovery. The seer, and to a lesser extent, the questioners, need time to return to ordinary consciousness. This was obviously easier when a journey of days or weeks was required to reach the seer in the first place, and people did not get into a car right after the ceremony and speed away. In our own work, we have found that even when the seer has not fasted before the ritual, oracular work uses calories, and it is wise to raise blood sugar and ground consciousness after the ritual with a hearty meal.

IV

QUESTIONS AND ANSWERS:
PAST AND PRESENT

I am sitting in the high seat, veil drawn down and eyes closed. With outer senses, I feel the night air whispering to the live oak trees that surround the fire circle at the Ancient Ways festival. The energy of those who have come for the session mingles with the spirit of the land. But all that is only a distant background to the dark lake and the black swan I see with my inner eyes. From somewhere in the outer darkness someone speaks—a young woman, nobody I know.

"Seeress, I've been working on a project for a long time, and I don't feel as if I'm getting anywhere. Should I give up on it and do something else?"

My guide speaks. "Say then, seeress, 'til said thou hast, answer the asker 'til all she knows—"

I want to stay in this shadowed peace, but the command compels me. With an effort, I rouse, but the dark water is all I see. I send out a silent call.

"Raven, give me some help—we're not here for our health, you know . . ."

She appears at my shoulder, flaps off toward the forest, and I follow. As I move along the path through the woods, the scene grows brighter.

"I see an open field. It's full of ripe grass." As I find words, the images become clear. "On the ground, among the stems, something is moving. I think it's a mouse . . ." I am surprised to hear subdued laughter from the people in the crowd. Fascinated, I let the vision unroll. "The mouse is scurrying around, collecting the grains that fall from above. I see her carrying them back to her hole. She has quite a pile. . . ." I wait, but sometimes the vision is all that comes, and I can only hope that it made sense to the querent, since it means nothing to me. Still, it's nice if I can add an interpretation.

"I think . . . this means that although you don't feel you are getting anywhere, you are actually making good progress, and you should keep on." I wait a moment, but there is no more information. "This you know. Would you know more?"

"No," comes the reply. "Thank you, seeress."

I sink back into the darkness, waiting for the next question.

Most of the time, the questions I receive and the answers I give fade as quickly as dreams. I am only the channel through which the information comes. I remember this exchange so vividly because after the session was over, the young woman who had asked the question came up to me and explained why her friends had laughed. She was a biologist, and for the past several years, she had been waitressing all winter to earn the money to support herself during the summer's fieldwork. She had been considering quitting, but now she was going to keep on.

Her subject was a study of rodents in grasslands.

She was quite impressed by my answer. So was I. Clearly, the only way I could have come up with that particular image was through telepathy. My interpretation was a piece of good advice that she might well have been given before, but because she received it in a ritual setting when her mind was open, she could *hear*. Though I articulated the answer, I think it came from her own soul, not from mine.

THE NEED FOR KNOWLEDGE

The age of oracles is not past. Although most modern seers do not work in a ceremonial setting, there is hardly a town or city without its resident psychics. Typing "Psychic Readers—Oakland, CA" in an Internet search engine pulls up *four pages* of listings. Admittedly, I live in the San Francisco Bay Area, where you can probably find at least one practitioner of any spiritual system ever known, but the listings for Kansas City are about the same. Some answer questions over the phone; some have offices. They read palms or cards, gaze into crystals, cast horoscopes. Some psychics have become celebrities, charging thousands for consultations. Or you can pay a dollar a minute for a Tarot reading at a psychic fair.

In *The Psychic Tourist*, William Little reports on his odyssey through Britain and the United States, seeking a psychic who can reliably predict the future. None of them succeed in giving *him* a completely correct prediction, but many of the people he talks to swear they have received good answers. Some of them use psychics as spiritual counselors, returning at regular intervals for further guidance. They ask about their health and their love lives, about life decisions and ways to help family members.

In one-on-one readings the psychic is generally in a state of divided consciousness in which she can carry on a conversation with the querent while asking questions that focus her search. Skeptics will say that probing questions also allow the psychic to gather information, but psychics also may simply fire off statements, such as a prediction of pregnancy or a change of career. Often they miss, but sometimes they are right on.

VOICES FROM THE PAST

Did the ancient oracles do any better than today's psychics? How do the responses of Apollo differ from those of Sylvia Browne or the seers of Seidhjallr today?

Delphi

Delphi was the most important oracle of the ancient world, and many of the questions and answers given there were recorded for posterity.

Diana Paxson at Delphi

According to Classical scholar Joseph Fontenrose, people brought questions about religious affairs, civic matters, and an assortment of domestic concerns. Advice on founding new cults, on festivals or temples, on praying to specific deities, and on religious laws and customs was preserved in the temples. Public concerns included commands or statements about rulers, legislation, and the foundation of colonies. The historicity of most domestic responses is impossible to prove, no doubt because they were primarily of interest to the people who asked the questions. For purposes of comparison, however, it is the domestic responses that offer the most productive data, since these are the kinds of questions usually asked today.

Whether or not the pythia sometimes got a boost from ethylene fumes, she spoke "clearly, coherently, and directly to the consultant in response to his question" (Fontenrose 1978, 10). The most common format for a Delphic answer was a simple command to perform a certain act in order to gain success or evade misfortune, or a statement saying that if the querent did something he would have success or avoid difficulties. Many historical answers of this type were confirmations sanctioning a proposed plan, such as building a temple.

However, some instructions are harder to understand. The classic example is the famous prophecy that if King Croesus of Lydia crossed the Halys River to attack the Persians, a great empire would fall. This will be discussed in more detail in Chapter VII. Some prophecies are contingent upon an event or omen. Sometimes the answer took the form of a prohibition, warning, or a simple statement, such as that no man was wiser than Socrates. There are also predictions in which a destined event will happen when an apparently unlikely condition is fulfilled. Answers might also come in the form of images, as when Philip of Macedon asked if he should attack Persia and was told, "The bull is garlanded; he comes to an end; the sacrificer is at hand."

Fontenrose identifies certain patterns in the way that the questions were asked, such as "Shall I do X?", "How shall I do X?", "What shall I do for X to happen?", "What should I do to please the gods?" or "To what god(s) shall I sacrifice (and pray)?", "Who or what was the cause of X?", "Whom should I or we choose?", "Where should I go or settle?", "Will I succeed in X?" "What is the truth about X?", and "Is it better to do this or that?" For example, when asked whether the Chalcidians should make an alliance with King Philip of Macedon, the oracle replied, "It is better that they become friends and allies according to the terms agreed upon" (Historical Answer 19). A Greek gentleman asked whether his wife would give him a child. Later, he recorded that "Phoibos granted progeny with his oracles, heeding my prayer, and he instructed me to make a hair-offering." Eleven months later, a daughter was born (Historical Answer 34), and the father offered the traditional first lock of hair. When the poet Pindar asked "What is best for man?" the god answered, "He himself knows, being the poet who wrote about Trophonios and Agamedes. But if he wants a test, it will soon be clear to him" (Quasi-historical Answer 179). This answer is of the type I call "Don't ask questions when you already know the answer."

Scandinavia

Of the forty-four references to seidh collected by James Chisholm from the Old Norse literature in *A Source-Book of Seidh*, six describe oracular sessions. In the *Saga of Erik the Red*, the main question is about when the current famine will end. In *Arrow-Odd's Saga*, the seeress forecasts the winter's weather. In both of these sagas, we are told that the seeress also answered a variety of questions for other people. In the *Saga of Erik the Red*, the völva also tells Gudrid about her marriages and future life. In *Nornagesttháttr*, a spákona is asked to foretell the future of the chieftain's child. In another episode, found in both *Hrolf Kraki's Saga* and the *Historia Danorum*, the king asks the völva to help him find two boys who are destined to be his enemies. As she begins to speak, the boys' secret supporters toss gold into her lap, and she tries to change her answer. It is no surprise that in all of these accounts the answers and foretellings are completely accurate, since they serve a literary purpose in the saga.

CONTEMPORARY QUESTIONS AND ANSWERS: THE SEIDHJALLR FILES

Since 1990, my group has been offering spae sessions in the San Francisco Bay Area, first at the Ancient Ways festival in the mountains of Lake County and then at Pantheacon, in a hotel in San Jose. At these sessions, we admit up to sixty participants, of whom around forty usually ask questions. In 2000, we began presenting smaller sessions four times a year at the Berkeley Fellowship of Unitarian Universalists hall, at which a dozen or so may attend. This more intimate setting sometimes allows us to delegate one of the team to take notes, which are stripped of names and posted to those who would like a record of the experience. Over a period of ten years, we have been able to record thirteen of these sessions.

These sessions are publicized through e-lists and fliers to the Bay Area pagan community. Attendees include people of all religious backgrounds, ages, and genders. The Seidh team consists of one or more seers, a guide, at least one warder, and if available, a scribe. Different team members act as seers, guides, and so on each time. Generally we have two seers, to make sure that everyone's questions get answered.

Question Categories with Examples

Total number of questions answered	149
1. General future	20
2. Work and income	26
3. Housing	2
4. Health and healing	11
5. Travel (usually work related)	7
6. Relationships (love, partnership)	8
7. Family members' problems	12
8. Friends' problems	5
9. Community problems	6
10. Spiritual choices	5
11. Interpreting dreams or omens	2
12. Questions for the Dead*	23
13. Questions for Gods and Goddesses*	32

*Ancestors and gods may be asked questions about relationships, work, etc.

The summary given above does not cover all of the sessions that took place over this period, nor does it include the larger sessions at Pantheacon or other festivals. But the kinds of questions being asked remain fairly constant. The figure for the number of questions asked should be considered approximate, as some answers stimulate further questions to explore the topic. When deities or the dead are questioned, the answer may turn into a conversation.

In the following examples, note the use of imagery, which can allow people to ask and be answered without sharing personal information with the rest of the group. Often even the seer does not actually know what the answer means.

Today, as in the past, people are concerned with their choices, their livelihood, and their relationships to other humans and to the gods.

1. General Future

One of the most consistently popular questions is a general query of the "Who am I and where am I going?" type. Sometimes the question proposes a choice, which may be expressed in imagery; other questions are more open-ended.

> **Questioner.** As long as I can remember I feel like I've been looking for something. All I find is the emptiness of its wake. Will I find it?
>
> **Seer.** Yes, but you would know more . . .
>
> **Questioner.** Do you know what I am looking for?
>
> **Seer.** Solid footing. You are wandering in the tide, not able to touch bottom. There it is. The sea is the faith, the understanding. It would be possible to float on it. It can carry you to shore. When you worry about it, you float farther out to sea, and you are wanting to hold your breath for a very long time, trying to touch bottom. If you learn to swim, if you find the path resonates well enough that you can gain purchase in faith, you can then direct your course to that land. Others can help you, but you have to do this. This you know.

2. Work and Income

The other topic that almost always comes up has to do with livelihood. People want to know where they can find work, whether they are doing the right work, what work they should do or where, or whether the work they are doing will prosper. Very often these questions involve choices.

> **Questioner.** The path before me is rather cloudy. I have a business venture I'm immersed in that is close to my heart, but I also see a destination far from here, where my heart lies. Is this path one or two, and which should I follow?

> **Seer.** I see two possible actions on your part. One is suddenly going out the door leaving it wide open, not even taking your coat, and starting down the path and finding when you arrive you don't have what you need for the journey to be profitable. The other is packing what you need and looking back and forth to the door, seeing the distance, and deciding what you need to take. It is a matter of timing. That is what is crucial—that you go carrying what you need to have when you arrive, and you watch the path of the sun so you arrive before it sets, but not too long.

Sometimes, however, we get hard information. Caitlin Matthews recalls the following anwer: "I gave exact directions to someone seeking a job after being made redundant. He asked where to look, and his answer was very precise: near a particular town, with a specific name and logo of the business. He subsequently applied there and was accepted."

3. Housing

Sometimes the answer comes in images, as above, while at other times the advice is more direct. Bob Fry recalls the following question:

> The last time I sat in the Chair, I remember that I got one querent who was asking about selling her house. I described a person who she needed to work with, adding that I saw her filled with spring energy and surrounded by ivy (or something similar). After the Seidh, the querent came up to me and showed me her Realtor's business card, touting "new beginnings" and showing the Realtor's picture edged with ivy.

4. Health and Healing

Questions regarding health are always challenging. This is one reason we emphasize that if the answer relates to a major decision, questioners should always get a second opinion. Fortunately, visions of disaster are rare, although there have been a few times when the seer saw something seriously wrong. This is one of the situations in which the seer has to decide whether to convey exactly what he or she sees or to simply suggest very strongly that the querent seek medical advice. Sometimes the answer is pretty obvious, but the querent needs to receive it in a state of mind in which it can be heard.

> **Questioner.** One of my friends recently had surgeries. Some things were mishandled afterwards. Should legal action be taken?
>
> **Seer.** The wronged ones should speak of this together. If the end results were of no great ill or due to no ill will, then no, but if there was spite or malice, then yes. Speak together with open hearts, and if the cause is just and energy is there, then go ahead. Means may be lean, but do not let that determine the course of action. Do not do it lightly or think it will be quick to resolve. Was there danger of the loss of a leg or foot? Risk is there, especially of a foot—small vessels need help to flow correctly. They need to be diligent with therapy and note when loss of feeling or wrongness of color is present. Medication must be taken despite [its] tedious nature. Prayer and effort are needed by the partner/priest to help with healing.

Bari Mandelbaum, who works as a medical intuitive practitioner as well as a seer, reports the following experience:

> There was a woman I worked with in whose blood I saw a dark cloudiness. I recommended she go for lab work, and sure enough, she was found to have a blood-borne parasite that could have gotten more serious if left untreated. That was the first time I had ever seen a health problem just with "oracle" eyes that was then confirmed by a medical diagnosis, and this was the client who gave me the confidence to further bring my spirit work into my professional practice.

5. Travel

Many questions about travel are work related, as in this example, in which the question as well as the answer are expressed in imagery. The answer tells the querent more about the situation and leaves him to decide which he prefers.

> **Questioner.** I am looking for work elsewhere. My path might lead me into the mountains or into the valley below. Which is the path I should take?

> **Seer.** I stand on top of the mountain, and I can see the valley and everything in it. The mountain is clean and cold; the valley is focused on itself.

6. Relationships

Another general category that always gets questions is relationships, especially involving love and partnership. Here are some examples.

> **Questioner.** Seer, I'd like to ask about my next relationship.

> **Seer.** There is a dark woman whom you will meet. She has experience, she has time, she has thought. Your steps move along together for a little while. Listen to this dark woman, but do not give everything you have to her, or she will take it and walk away. She comes to you because you are young and because you have something she wants. She has something to teach you. Listen with your heart. Would you know more?

> **Questioner.** Yes. What should I do now?

> **Seer.** Be available.

7 and 8. Problems of Family Members and Friends

Sometimes people ask for advice on how to help those they love.

With all questions, the seers are trained to signal the end of an answer with a phrase based on the responses in some of the Old Norse poems. In a small group, there is time for the questioner to ask additional questions that can amplify the answer.

> **Questioner.** What is it that my son is hearing? Does it come from within or without?

> **Seer.** He needs training far beyond his years; he needs context. I have this image of a funnel into him, explaining calculus when you only understand addition. He needs to understand why it is he is here. Internal commentary is mixed with it. He needs a translator for something that only he hears. It will be difficult. This you know.

> **Questioner.** Can you clarify? Is part of his current manifestation because he is actually picking up from those around him?

> **Seer.** Those here, those beyond—there is so much about him. It is a concert hall five minutes before it starts; everyone talking, attempting to hear all the conversations.

In a community, the problems of one are the problems of all. The vividness of the answer often depends on the degree of need in the question.

> **Questioner.** I have a friend whose son through his teens was in trouble with the law. He is now twenty and going through changes. What's going to happen and what can she do about it?

> **Seer.** Has he learned his lessons? If he has not learned his lessons, he will have problems again. Nothing you can do will help. He must be left to be an adult, to learn. The only way to protect him is to tie him up. If he doesn't learn how to not do wrong or how not to get caught, he'll stay on this path. I see him less learning how not to get caught and more getting caught.

> **Questioner.** Can his mother do anything to help?

> **Seer.** When they are that age, they do not want to listen to their mothers. He will learn from the handcuffs, not from her.

9. Community Problems

People also ask about problems with groups in which they are involved.

> **Questioner.** Seer, there is discord in my lodge. What counsel can you give me on that?

> **Seer.** There are leaks in the house, holes in the floor. You wander through, patching and binding. You may as well remake the house, for more than that is what you're putting into this. This you know. Would you know more?

> **Questioner.** The one who leads the lodge, what wisdom do you have for that person?

> **Seer.** Those that are true had better stand together in the wilderness. Do not discard those that don't fit, but know who your alliance is with so that you can be true.

10. Spiritual Choices

At almost every festival, we will get a question that boils down to "What's my path?" Initially, I thought that this was one question that would never have been asked in the old days, since Greeks and Icelanders knew what religion they belonged to, but it seems to me that the people who asked the Delphic oracle what gods they should make offerings to or build a temple for were getting at essentially the same thing. When faced with today's spiritual smorgasbord, making choices can be difficult. Rather than prescribing a choice, the seer advises the querent how to choose.

> **Questioner.** I ask about my own ancestry and the spiritual path I'm following. Is it the one for me?

> **Seer.** I have feet; you have feet. When there are so many paths to choose from, as there are in this time and place, the path you take is the one you make. If you choose the ancestral path, that is well; if another calling is the path of your heart, that is the path. The goal

of the path is important; not all are the same, but there's not a great number. The definition of the path is the journey you make along it, and the definition of yourself is the journey you take. Seek the ancestral path or not, but all paths are good that lead you to examine your place in the universe. Any path that requires you to hand all yourself over to another is no good. I am here to tell you to enjoy the journey; after that, all is detail.

11. Interpreting Dreams or Omens

Some of the more interesting questions have to do with the interpretation of material from the querent's own spiritual work.

Questioner. Recently on a (trance) journey, I asked a favor of any deity who was willing to help me and assist me. I was at an altar at which I provided three stones. A hooded figure came and took the stones without a word. I did not get the impression it was someone I was familiar with, or even Norse, but very powerful. It took the stones and left. Since then I have been attempting to find out more. Do you have some insight?

Seer. Part of the repayment of the favor is discovering the nature of the entity. Most gods are shape-shifters, and any may put on a cloak. So don't limit yourself to what is familiar. Your voyage to understand its identity will teach you much about yourself and help you to stand on your feet and help you when you may speak with it. I see the hand and cloak and a smile, but I am not allowed to tell you more.

12. Questions for the Dead

Given that most of our questioners come from the pagan community, in which the late autumn is a time to honor the dead, our November seidh sessions often include a lot of questions for departed friends and relatives. However, the kinds of answers we get from spirits differ from those we receive directly. For this reason, I will be giving examples of such interactions in Chapter V, "Sources and Spirits."

13. Questions for Gods and Goddesses

Like the dead, the gods have their own opinions and agendas. When someone wishes to consult a deity, the seer usually journeys in spirit to another part of the Otherworld. Sometimes answers are relayed, while at other times, the deity takes over and answers directly. These answers will also be discussed in Chapter V.

Feedback

I have often been tempted to run exit polls after an oracular session, in hopes of learning how many people thought the answers they received were accurate and useful. The fact that we have capacity crowds at Pantheacon year after year suggests that people are getting something out of the experience. One woman told me she never asked a question—she just enjoyed the energy. But for most people, the attraction is clearly the opportunity to get information or sometimes to observe a dramatic interaction between the seer and someone else.

Aside from the woman who at one session proclaimed loudly as she left that the seer's answer was "all wrong!" (despite the fact that her friends had been nodding as it was given), we rarely hear from those who disagreed with the seers' words. Nor do we necessarily hear about the successful answers. When a questioner gasps and starts to weep after hearing her answer, we can assume that the seer said something relevant, but only when someone tells us what it was all about do we know what an answer means.

We always tell people to seek a second opinion when the question is critical. Hearing that another seer has confirmed the answer is particularly encouraging. This example comes from Galina Krasskova:

> One reading stands out. (I later found out that the querent had gone to three different diviners and independently of each other, [and] all three of us had given the same answer.) . . . [T]he answers given helped a man put to rest some very painful issues he had surrounding an abusive parent. He was able to find closure in a way that turned out to be very, very productive and healthy for him.

Sometimes answers that seemed trivial turn out to be vitally important. Jordsvin, a spámadhr working in Kentucky, forwarded this e-mail to me with the subject header, "This seidhr was a life saver!" from Sandra L., who had attended one of his sessions.

> Hi, Jordsvin tells me you are interested in the story behind the following image (of a mechanic's report indicating that the tie rod on the front wheels was about to give way, which would have taken out the steering).
>
> I was at a seidhr where he [Jordsvin] was sitting in the high seat on a Saturday night. I had told him that I would have to leave early to get to work. As I was quietly trying to slip away, he told me to stop, that there was a message for me. He said that a short round woman who looked like an Indian wanted to tell me something. He said she was smoking a pipe. He said that he could see them traveling across the country in a covered wagon. The message was, "The squeaky wheel gets the grease." He repeated this message several times.
>
> I knew my great grandparents had indeed traveled in a covered wagon, because my mother had ridden in it as a child. I believe I had mentioned this bit of trivia to Jordsvin. But what was surprising is that I am sure I never told him about my great grandmother's pretty blue and white flowered china pipe! I am 57 now, and I clearly remember my great grandmother smoking that pipe.
>
> Well, as I drove home that night, I thought about my van and the funny noises I sometimes heard from the wheel. The next day was Sunday. I didn't go anywhere, but I determined to have the car looked at when the garage across the street opened on Monday. Imagine my feelings when I got back the enclosed report! That seidhr probably saved my life and the life of my son!

When the need is truly great, the seer may not even have to hear the question to get an accurate answer. Rod Landreth reports:

> Apparently, I started answering a person's question quite clearly once before they even got in front of me to ask. I was so vehement and dead on that they claimed I actually frightened them.

At one session when Laurel (who works closely with the goddess Freyja, who likes cats) was in the chair, she suddenly announced that the house owner's cat wanted to be scratched in a particular place. Afterward we were told that their other cat had recently died. The two cats used to groom each other, and the dead cat had taken care of the spot that the living cat, who was missing a leg, could not reach.

How often do our modern seers give accurate answers? Without formal data, there is no way to know. The "Jeanne Dixon effect" predisposes us to remember the successful answers more vividly. I doubt that any seer or psychic, including those with whom I work, bats a thousand. The feedback we do receive indicates that we are succeeding often enough to carry on.

Crafting the Question

In the course of listening to hundreds of answers, we have come to realize that the skill of the seer is only part of the equation. The success of the answer can also depend on the question. Some kinds of questions consistently seem to get more effective answers, while for others, the results are often uninspired.

One thing that seems to make a difference is the degree of *need*. In the ancient world, no one made the trip to Delphi or one of the other oracular centers unless they really cared about the answer. When a question has a lot of emotion behind it, the energy is stronger, and it becomes easier for the seer to make a good connection.

When a querent is accompanied by a support group of friends who are also concerned, the answers come with even greater power. Conversely, when the question has clearly been asked on the spur of the moment or because everyone else is asking, the seer may find it difficult to get a "fix" on the energy and come up with anything significant. Obviously frivolous questions, such as "What kind of ice cream did I have at dinner tonight?" (this actually happened), deserve, and usually receive, a smackdown from the seer.

As Dianne Skafte points out in her advice on how to get the best results when visiting a psychic, "Many practitioners are not good at picking up names, dates, and other concrete facts. But they may be able to reach to the heart of a problem and help you in ways that are very important. The best way to evaluate a practitioner's quality is to ask yourself,

'Is this person giving me information, guidance, or illumination that really feels on target and seems useful to me?'" (Skafte 2000, 94). I would agree. In particular, numbers seem hard to identify. Asking for the winning Lotto number might get you a good number, but without the right date, it's not very useful.

It is also important to keep the question focused. If the querent asks if she'll find a new partner, the seer can zero in. Adding, "And will we stay together and will I have children?" expands the target area to include too many variables. We tell questioners to limit the first query and wait until it has been answered to ask more.

V

SOURCES AND SPIRITS

"Seeress, can I ask a question of Freyja?"

The question comes to me through the comfortable darkness in which I rest after the previous question. I rouse to awareness of the shadowy underworld around me. But this is not a place where the goddess is likely to be found.

"Yes, but not here," I reply. I feel my shape changing, feel the stretch and pull of black-feathered wings as I follow my guide up from the depths, around the Tree, up and around until I am flying over the plain of Midgard. Below me, field and forest unroll in vivid variety until I see the blue shimmer of the sea and the tree-clothed shape of the island.

"Vanaheim is before me, blooming and beautiful. The air is rich with the scent of growing things. I fly over orchards heavy with fruit and the gold of ripe fields. And now there's a clearing where warriors and maidens are danc-ing around a fire."

I settle to the earth and take my own form once more. There seems to be a party going on. Food is cooking in a cauldron hung over the coals. To one side is a wicker chariot. As I look around, my gaze is drawn to a woman who sits on a chair carved from a log.

"I see the Lady. She is tall and fair, dressed in green, with hair the red gold of the fire. Next to her the flames look dim. Now she notices me and smiles. What would you ask of her?"

"My cat just died. I had him since he was a kitten—." There is a catch in the woman's voice, and I hear a murmur as her friends comfort her. She coughs and goes on, "I just want to know is he all right? Does Freyja have him there?"

"I see her standing up," I reply. "She's smiling. She stretches out her hand." Two big orange tabbies wait expectantly by a table where a man is slicing meat. Are they the two that pull that chariot I saw? Actually, I see lots of cats; now that I'm looking, they seem to be everywhere, sunning themselves,

begging for food, hunting among the trees. And then I feel a soft pressure against my leg.

"There's a black and white tuxedo cat stropping my ankles—"

"Oh, that's Mr. Bojangles! That's him!"

"Freyja says she heard when you asked her to take care of him. She's saying that he will be fine with her until it's time for him to come back again. But don't wait for him—" More knowledge comes to me. "The message I'm getting from the cat is that he taught you all he could and now he needs to go on and so should you. I think this means that you should get a new kitten. Does that make sense to you?"

"Yes . . .," the voice is very soft. "I was going to, but then it felt disloyal. Yes."

"Freyja says you took good care of him. You did everything you should. Your cat loves you, and so does she. She says you will find your next cat at the shelter. Give them a donation in your kitty's name." I can hear weeping, but it is the good kind that releases sorrow. The goddess sits down, and the cat has wandered away. "That's all she has to say to you now."

I take raven form again and rejoin my ally, who has been waiting in a tree. Together we return to the Underworld. I sink into the comforting darkness and wait for the next question to come.

As we have seen, the answers people give when in an oracular trance vary widely. But where do these answers come from? Before the seer opens the door to knowledge, she or he needs to know that its source will do no harm. To correctly gauge the value of the information, the questioner must be able to trust that its source has his or her best interests at heart.

SOURCES

The more glamorous the source—whether it's a god, ascended master, or noble Indian chief—the more impressive the communication and the easier it is to believe. Oracles in different times and places have depended on a variety of sources, and as we have seen, there are certain similarities in the kinds of answers they give.

The seers I surveyed encounter and get information from a variety of places, depending on the question. Sometimes an answer arrives as pure knowledge or is perceived as a vision. If they seek answers through journeying, they may travel to the Well of Wyrd, the spirit world, or settings drawn from various mythologies. Often, however, the seer moves through a protean environment variously characterized as the web of the universe, Wyrd, the collective unconscious, the ether, or even the mind of the querent. When a question is directed to the dead or a god, we go to them for answers. However, when the question is not so directed, a being is less likely to be cited.

Whatever the source, "By their fruits ye shall know them" (Matthew 7:16) is still a good way to judge the source of an answer.

GOOD NEWS FROM THE GODS

The idea that gods can speak to or through men is found in many cultures. In the Graeco-Roman tradition, all oracles came from the gods. When the seeress appears at the beginning of Aeschylus' *The Eumenides* I:i, (quoted at the beginning of Chapter I), she lists the deities who have given oracles, ending with Apollo, who himself speaks for Zeus.

Apollo was not the only deity who could give oracles, but he eventually became the most popular. When followers of the Hellenic tradition do oracle work today, he is the one from whom the words come. Iamblichus observes, "[W]hen she [the pythia] sits down in the seat of the god she comes into harmony with the unwavering oracular power of the divinity, and from these two preparatory operations she becomes entirely the medium of the god" (*De Mysteriis*, 3.7).

However, except in the *Aeneid* VI, in which Apollo descends upon the oracle of Cumae, the sources do not indicate that the god actually possessed the oracle; instead, he only spoke through her.

Across times and traditions we find a continuum of trance states, ranging from relaying the information through channeling to complete possession, in which the personality of the seer is replaced by that of the god. Now, as in ancient Greece, people want to know what their gods require of them. When people ask such questions in our own oracular ceremonies, the usual response is to seek the deity and relay his or her answer, as in the example at the beginning of this chapter. However, some of our seers are also trained in deity possession, and when a question, or especially more than one question, is addressed to a deity the seer works with, it is often much simpler for the god to drop in and answer directly. In our community, the deities most often called are Freyja and Odin.

This example, from a session held the week before a devotional ritual in honor of Odin, shows what can happen.

> **Questioner 1.** I would ask a question of Odin, if he's available. Are there any words on preparations for the party?

> **Seeress.** Arrange the glasses so he will not knock them over. Be sure that there is enough space. He seems to be in a mood of high energy, of anticipating. He looks forward to a great deal of physical movement as he interacts with those who hear his words. His main concern is that (he wishes I'd take him on, but I'd rather relay his words) he wants space to move and to not have to be concerned with delicate obstacles.

> **Questioner 2.** I'd like to ask Odin—On the long road are there near-term missteps that I can avoid judiciously?

> **Seeress.** All right, *fine!*" [The seeress gives in and lets Odin take over. She pushes back the veil and shifts position, leaning on one elbow on the arm of the chair, head cocked, and one eye closed, and we hear Odin's deep, characteristic laugh.]

> **Odin.** Sometimes a rough ride makes it more interesting. If it's too smooth, people fall asleep and fall off the trail. You don't have to worry about all the rocks, missteps, holes—only the large ones. And you are well situated to notice boulders and trees in the way. So long as you keep your eyes on the road and pay attention to those and the sound of paws and the whispering of wind, you will do well, though it may be a bit more bumpy than you would like. Is there anything else you'd like to know?"

> **Questioner.** Do those traveling alongside me know what they're in for?

> **Odin.** They know that walking alongside you is a mixture of delight and doom, and they choose to accompany you willingly.

Each seer has a characteristic body language when in the chair, and most answers are given in a measured, dispassionate tone, directly, without emotional involvement. When a deity drops in, however, the answer is given from his or her point of view, in a distinctive tone of voice, and reflects his opinion. This may or may not be the best answer to the question.

Sometimes the gods don't have to speak to make their point, as in this story from Winifred Hodge Rose.

> A rather Goth-looking young woman said she felt things weren't quite right between herself and Odin, and wanted to know what he thought she should do. So Odin appeared before me on a sunny beach, wearing a ridiculous-looking Hawaiian-tourist, flowered shirt; baggy shorts that showed his knobbly knees; a "wizard" hat; floppy sandals; and sunglasses below his big, bushy eyebrows, which he waggled constantly. All of us, myself included, couldn't help laughing at this image; then Freyja showed up, and she and he started telling each other silly jokes and nudging each other.
>
> After a bit of this, I asked Odin more specifically what he suggested for the querent, and he said, "I'm *trying* to make her *laugh* more!" At that very moment, we heard a tapping, and a voice whispering "Help! I'm stuck" came from the bathroom next to the living room where the session was being held. Someone had gone quietly in to use it, then when he tried to exit, the door handle came off in his hand, just like in a slapstick comedy. We all laughed ourselves to tears. Odin got his way!

When a deity drops in during a session, the energy goes up, and people who had run out of questions may suddenly think of things they want to ask. However, if a querent is asking because he thinks it would be fun to have a conversation rather than because this is a good question for that particular deity—as happened when a woman asked Odin for help in getting pregnant and he answered that he had a hall full of warriors who could reincarnate in her womb—the answer is less successful. I have come to believe that unless the question has to do specifically with the questioner's relationship with the deity or lies specifically within the deity's area of concern, it is better to ask for answers from the seer than from the gods.

SPEAKERS FOR THE DEAD

In both Classical literature and Norse and Celtic lore, the gods are not the only ones who give answers. People in many cultures have sought out the dead for counsel.

Journeys to Hades

One of the earliest Classical accounts of a search for supernatural advice occurs in Homer's *Odyssey* (XI:488–91), in which the only one who can tell Odysseus how to get home is the Theban seer Tiresias, who is, unfortunately, dead. However, Circe has told the hero how to reach the shores of Hades and what to do when he arrives. Where the smoke from the burning offerings was sufficient for the gods, the dead need the energy in the blood of the sacrifices in order to "talk with you like a reasonable being." Tiresias tells Odysseus about the hazards that still stand before him and says that he will reach home with or without his men, depending on their choices.

In the *Aeneid,* the hero, whose father's ghost has been speaking to him in dreams, consults the Sibyl. But instead of conveying an answer from Apollo, she leads Aeneas to an entrance to Hades by Lake Avernus, where, protected by the golden bough, he enters the Underworld and receives his father's counsel.

While everyone has heard of the divine oracles at places like Delphi, what is less well-known is the existence of at least two *necromanteions*— temple complexes at which querents moved through an underground reconstruction of Hades in order to reach a chamber in which they could put their questions to the spirits. It must have been rather like going through a haunted house at Hallowe'en, except that the setting, and perhaps the ingestion of psychotropic herbs, put the querent into a state in which he either could hear the spirits himself or priests who were speaking the spirits' words.

One of these oracles of the dead was in Thesprotia, on the west coast of northern Greece, and the other was at Baiae, near Naples, on the west coast of Italy. The Thesprotian oracle site has been excavated. The one at

THE WAY OF THE ORACLE

Baiae was rediscovered in 1962 by Robert Paget, and although Robert Temple explored further in 2001, there has never been a full excavation. His findings are described in *Oracles of the Dead*.

By the time Virgil wrote the *Aeneid*, the oracular site at Cumae had been replaced by a temple to Apollo, but the necromanteion at Baiae may have still been in operation. Temple believes that it inspired Homer's description of Hades. The site in Greece was surrounded by dismal swamps and imposing mountains, while the waters of Lake Avernus near Naples still reflect dark forests, and sulfurous fumes and boiling springs provide all the hellish effects one might need.

Severed Heads and Sacred Mounds

Despite the misty and melancholic images of modern fantasy, the early Celts were a vigorous and often bloody-minded people, notable for, among other things, collecting as trophies the heads of their enemies. Folktales from the Hebrides include episodes in which a head speaks. In the *Mabinogion*, the head of the supernatural king Bran is carried about by his companions, prophesying and entertaining them. We find another example in the story of Fionn MacCumhal, when the severed head of Lomna the Fool, who has been killed by Coirpre for betraying his adultery with Fionn's wife, foretells his murderer's doom.

The Celtic tradition may also have inspired the story of Mímir, who was given by one group of Norse gods as hostage to another after their war and beheaded when the latter were disappointed in his counsel. In the *Ynglingasaga*, Snorri Sturlusson tells us that "Odin took the head, smeared it with herbs so that it should not rot, and sang incantations over it. Thereby he gave it the power that it spoke to him, and discovered to him many secrets" (*Ynglingasaga* 4). And "Odin carried with him Mime's head, which told him all the news of other countries. Sometimes even he called the dead out of the earth, or set himself beside the burial-mounds; whence he was called the ghost-sovereign, and lord of the mounds" (*Ynglingasaga* 7). In stanza 157 of the *Havamál*, Odin also boasts of using rune magic to compel a hanged man to speak to him.

The dead may also be summoned to speak from their grave mounds. In *Svipdagsmál*, a young man cursed by his evil stepmother to seek the unattainable maiden Mengloth goes to his own mother's mound for counsel. His mother's spirit proceeds to give him several pages of good advice on how to survive the dangers he will face on his way to court the maiden. In European folklore, dead mothers often serve as guardian spirits or become the fairy godmothers of fairy tales. Once their own children are grown, they apparently merge into the ranks of the *dísir*, the maternal spirits who watch over the family line. What Svipdag does in this passage is called *utiseta*, "sitting out" in the wilderness or at a grave mound.

As in the Classical world, in Norse lore the dead can also be reached by journeying to the Underworld. It may seem redundant to find a grave mound in Hel, the realm of the dead, but the procedure that Odin follows clearly reflects the practice. When Odin's son Baldr begins to have ominous dreams, his father goes looking for information:

> *Odin rode on. The ground thundered,*
> *and he came to the high hall of Hel.*
> *Then Odin rode for the eastern door*
> *for he knew the tomb of the volva was there.*
> *Wise in witchcraft, he began to sing valgaldr*
> *until the corpse was forced to rise and speak.*

The Dream of Baldr 3–4

Spiritualism and Spiritism

It was not until the nineteenth century that a tradition developed in which the dead were the primary source of information for all topics, although they usually spoke about the afterlife and the spirit world. The spiritualist movement started in 1848 when two sisters in upstate New York, Kate and Margaret Fox, began getting messages from the spirit of a murdered peddler through rappings. As the movement spread, trance mediums emerged who channeled the words of the spirits directly or through "controls," advanced spirits who had taken on this duty to help humanity. Especially successful and charismatic mediums became trance lecturers, who worked on stage for large audiences, manifesting mental phenomena such as automatic and inspirational writing and drawing, possession by spirits, clairvoyance, clairaudience, prevision, and psychometry. Some sessions featured physical phenomena such as levitation and apportation, materializations of spirit forms, exudation of ectoplasm, and luminescent effects. Although some of the manifestations were proved fraudulent, other mediums made converts of the scientists who set out to debunk them. Nonetheless, the power of the movement was not primarily due to the phenomena, but rather to the message of love and faith transmitted through the mediums and the spiritualists' support for social causes such as abolition and women's rights.

According to W. H. Evans, mediums and psychics both work with the energy body, but while the medium is a passive vehicle for messages from the spirits, the psychic has conscious control of his powers. Most people have some capacity for mediumship, but do not demonstrate it until they begin to work with the spirit controls, who induce trance in their human friends in much the same way as a hypnotist. The spirits are mostly beneficent, but "The idea that death makes one omniscient is a mistaken one. We have to bring what we are told to the bar of our reason. ... On no account should we get into the habit of depending upon advice from those over the border. We are here to grow" (Evans c. 1950, 34). The medium generally has no awareness of what is said in the transmissions. Seances use prayer, music, and candlelight to create the conditions conducive to contact.

During the latter part of the nineteenth century, spiritualism acquired millions of adherents, especially in the United States and Great Britain. The desire of those bereaved during the Civil War and later during World War I to contact those they had lost no doubt increased the audience. Europe and South America saw a variant called spiritism, popularized by a French priest who wrote as Alain Kardec. In Brazil, the fusion of spiritism with African traditions produced the contemporary religion of Umbanda, in which the powers honored include the orixas (functional equivalents of gods), the *caboclos* (the spirits of native Indians), and the *pretos velhos* (the spirits of old black slaves). One of the services provided by the *Umbandistas* to the community is the *consulto*, in which mediums answer the same kinds of questions that are put to psychics and oracles.

In traditions inspired by spiritualism, it is assumed that the dead are the best source of answers. The personality of the spirit, like the personality of a deity, colors the style of the answer, but the actual information is similar to the sort of thing one would hear from a seer.

Prayers and Pot Roast: Socializing with Our Dead

Although the dead are not the primary source of information in Seidh-jallr's practice, in most sessions there will be a few questions, especially at those sessions held in early November, the season of the dead. Pagan theology allows for a number of possible afterlives. The Norse Hel is not a place of punishment, but the general destination for at least a portion of the soul (some theories hold that our "souls" may be a system of parts that have different destinations). It seems to be a good place to find people, even if they may also be somewhere else. Ever since the evening when a recently deceased friend tried to use the seeress to continue the argument he had been having with the woman who had asked after him, we have requested that questioners only ask to speak with spirits who have been dead at least a year. We feel that both we and they have to get used to the idea that they are gone.

Beyond the name and date of death we don't ask for details. Sometimes the spirit requested appears quickly and is happy to talk. Sometimes we contact what might be the spirit, but he or she is not interested in communication. Sometimes the spirit has apparently gone on or perhaps reincarnated, but other spirits crowd forward, eager to advise. We also warn people that "just because they're dead doesn't mean they're smart."

Sometimes the dead can be very chatty.

> **Questioner.** Seeress, I journey to the place of my birth soon. I would wish to ask a question of my mother.

> *(The seer takes a few moments to look.)*

> **Seer.** She says it's going to be cold and there will be bad weather. Be warm. Bring things to keep you warm, especially gloves. Protect your head, hands, and legs especially. Too many people have hurt legs; it's as though there's some spirit tripping folk in the community. I know you're stubborn and think you know everything, but get shoes that will not slip, for the weather will be bad. And don't stand under any trees because they will get heavy under the weight of snow and ice and fall on you, not to mention the power lines. What is your question? I feel she will go on like this for quite some time. Does this sound like her?

Questioner. Yes. (Some chuckling from the crowd.) May I visit my birthplace? Will anyone be there?

Seer. They may not be there, but go. Dress nicely, dress warmly, be careful walking on the sidewalks. Tell them you used to live there. Bring them a picture of yourself as a young boy in front of the house so they know you're not some freak coming to kill them. She says to make her something, I don't understand the word—not something you've made before, something new. Teach someone else. There is something small in the hand you have to make.

We later figured out that what the questioner was to make were pirogies, the potato- and cheese-stuffed semicircular dumpling so popular in Poland and other Eastern European countries.

Clearly, food is a powerful connection. Often, when someone asks how to get in touch with a relative, the seer will recommend making their favorite food, as in this example:

Questioner. My ancestors on my father's side call me strongly. What do they want from me?

Seer. This is a question for you to answer for yourself. Is there a favorite food from that line?

Questioner. No, but there's a style they like: meat and potatoes.

Seer. The answer I am getting is the taste of really excellent pot roast. Cook one for them. Not too fancy—plain-people food. It's the means to the end. You ask them to help you pick out the right cut of meat, the best carrots. When you make this, before you feed yourself and your beloved, set aside a plate for them. During the meal, don't talk among yourselves [more than necessary], but address yourself to them, talk to them. You are being invited to call them and say hello. It may turn out not to be a meal, but a conversation.

What was interesting about this answer was that as she spoke, not only the seeress, but also everyone else on the team was overwhelmed by the scent and taste of pot roast, unctuous, rich, redolent of good seasonings—a sort of culinary contact high.

There have been some other memorable questions for which we have no transcript. In particular, I remember a young man asking if the seer could find his father, who had died when he was young. His question for his father was "Why?" The seer's description of the man who came forward was confirmed by the querent. She then relayed the message that the father had to go because it would have been worse for the family if he had stayed. Afterward, the querent told us that his father had been a Vietnam war vet with serious post-traumatic stress disorder (PTSD) who had eventually killed himself. Our conclusion was that he had done it to protect his family from his own violence. The querent in this case was a stranger to us, and there was no way that the seer could have known any of this history.

In another session, a young woman was trying to find out more information about her birth mother. The seeress replied that she could see a beautiful red gemstone and then asked if the name "Miller" meant anything. One of the possible names that the girl was researching turned out to be "Ruby Miller."

Sometimes, communications with the dead can bring great comfort to the living. At one session, a woman who had lost her husband had asked a friend to see if he could be contacted, even though she herself doubted the existence of an afterlife. When the seeress went looking, some of the other sensitives shared her experience of reaching down into the darkness and pulling up a bouquet of violets surrounding one white rose, which the spirit of the husband said was a gift to his wife. When the friend who had asked the question passed on the information, the widow burst into tears. Her husband had given her just such a bouquet, which had a special and private meaning for them. The existence of this bouquet was known neither to the seer nor to anyone else in the room.

Other seers also report dramatic experiences of this kind. Jennifer Culver recalls, "At a rite specifically for ancestor communication, one answer was given to a man who had been troubled with nightmares. I was able to 'see' events at his father's funeral and describe certain elements in such a way that he was able to find peace and closure. His nightmares of this nature ceased."

Two other interesting accounts come from Patricia Lafayllve:

> I was speaking about someone's father (deceased) and his interactions with their child. I described the corner he stood in, what he looked like, and how he felt (the most amazing, deep, passionate

pride). Afterward the querent said I had gotten everything right—they'd seen their child (a pre-speech toddler) babbling into precisely that corner, then smiling as if listening, etc. The only thing I got wrong was the father's hair color, which is the kind of thing that can happen, and I said so. Later that day, the querent came to find me, white-faced. They'd called their mother and asked what their father looked like—and I was the one who was correct. The querent had remembered the hair color wrong. That gave us all chills.

More recently, a person asked me to contact their mother. I had a very hard time tracking her down, and she avoided answering me. The querent shot out a series of demanding questions—I remember their tone but not their words. There was a sudden shift, and I started giving answers. They were not the most polite ones, either, which always makes me a little nervous. Afterward, the person told me that I had absolutely contacted their mother and, in fact, had said a lot of the things she always said in life. It was a powerful, conflict-ridden, emotionally charged session, and I knew it needed to happen, even though it was one of the hardest ones I've experienced. The comfort I took then was that I had at least contacted the right ancestor, and I might have helped the querent gain some resolution.

That's the thing, with the power answers. I often have no recollection whatsoever of the original question asked or even of the specific words of the answer. I remember the thrust of the thing, the power of the thing, the immediacy of the thing. But it's there, and it's strong, and it changes people.

When a specific ancestor is contacted, it is often the physical details that are the most compelling, as in this example from Winifred Hodge Rose:

This involved a woman whom I'd met and briefly chatted with prior to the session, but I knew nothing at all about her family history. Her father had died, and she felt [there were] some unresolved issues with him that she wanted to hear from him about, though she said nothing of what these were.

I saw a man dressed in loose slacks and a sleeveless undershirt, with a dish towel tucked into his belt as an apron. He was neat and clean but had not shaved, and there was a blue parakeet sitting on his shoulder, talking into his ear and flying around. The man cooked stir-fry in a wok, then turned and served it to two teenaged girls sitting at a table nearby. He slowly and carefully made sure that each girl had a completely full plate, then showed us that there was plenty more left in the pan.

I described all this, and the woman started crying. She said that was exactly what her father used to do: he liked to cook and hated to dress formally and shave on the weekends; stir-fry was his favorite dish to cook, which he had learned to do while abroad in military service. He always tucked a dish towel into his slacks since an apron would look sissy, and they had a blue parakeet that was sometimes allowed to fly out of its cage. The other teenaged girl was her cousin, who had come to live with them for an extended time during their teens, and the woman had always worried that her father loved his niece better than his daughter. The symbolism used by the father to express his love was beautiful: he made sure each girl had all the food/love her plate could hold, and there was plenty left over for more. Everyone was very moved by this, and the woman felt that a long-standing self-doubt was healed.

All of these examples show something that usually happens when my spaework involves dead kin or friends. Usually the spirits show some kind of detail that would be very hard to guess or make up, and that serves as an identity-check. The querent can hear/see it and feel assured that we're talking to the right person. In this case, it was . . . the personal idiosyncrasies of the father.

However, people also get advice from the dead who are not a particular ancestor.

Questioner. I wish to be healthy, energetic, and healed.

Seeress. There is an old monk here who says, "You, seeress, know an answer! One of my order who still lives has written a wonderful book about things that will help her. You must tell her that one of my brothers in the order is very famous and is in the order. You know him, get her to read this book." [It turned out this was a book about gluten-free bread, I think.] I thank the good brother and go on looking. I see a table laid out. I see roast meats. I see vegetables and fruits of all sorts. There are people there. They have advice about your heart. They say sorrow in your heart is holding you back as much as your ill health. Does this make sense to you?"

Questioner. Yes.

Seeress. They would speak to you if you would give them food and drink and listen to them in silence. (She describes a Dumb Supper for a while.) Sit and light a single candle and listen to them. This Dumb Supper, if you will, will guide you in the healing of your heart and of half your woes.

Not all attempts to contact the dead are this successful. Some seers find it easier to make the connection than others, and not all the dead are willing to be found. Our experience has been that sometimes the spirit who has been requested is ready and eager to communicate, while others are present but uninterested in talking. When that happens, however, there are often other spirits who are happy to volunteer.

It should also be noted that just because they're dead doesn't mean they are nice. Although those with some connection to the querent are almost always happy to be contacted, other spirits may not be so friendly, and very rarely a spirit may try to latch on to the seer and follow him back to the world of the living, resulting in a haunting or obsession. This is one of the many reasons not to do this work alone. The seer's own spirit ally or a guardian figure associated with the oracle site can provide protection. The other members of the oracle team, especially the guide, can also sense the status of the seer and, during or after the trance, provide psychic first aid.

SPIRIT HELPERS

When Gudrid sings the *vardhlokkur* in the *Saga of Erik the Red*, the singing attracts "many spirits." The nature of these spirits is not defined, but clearly they are the source of the information the völva provides regarding the famine and other matters. With the exception of spirits in the

Saga of Erik the Red, a source for the völva's answers is not mentioned in the Old Norse literature.

In both the sagas and Scandinavian folklore we find references to a spirit called the *fylgja*, which accompanies a person either as a guardian or an aspect of the self, rather like the daemons in Philip Pullman's novel *The Golden Compass*. This concept may be a survival of the belief in helping animals or allies familiar from the shamanic literature. Although it is not clear whether the seidh workers of the Viking Age had spirit helpers in animal form, the neo-shamanic movement popularized the concept, and such allies are part of the practice of many of those who do oracular or psychic work today. Rod Landreth says,

> I do call my fylgia, a large gray wolf, to sort of be beside me, both to assist and to help me handle anything that isn't in the positive category. I also can draw strength from her, and her from me. When I have to do some sort of journeying, I have Bright Eyes to guide me. She takes me pretty directly to wherever I need to go. She also likes to go to places she has never been before. When I do straight spae . . ., Wolf is there but more as a support presence than really anything more than that.

When I first began exploring shamanic work, I picked up several "allies." I first encountered Raven at one of Michael Harner's workshops and initially resisted the connection on the grounds that half the pagan community was named "Raven" or had a raven totem. (In *Trance-Portation*, I have told that story in full.) Raven led me to Odin, who in turn led me to the research that resulted in the revival of a Norse-style oracular practice. When other people in our group also began encountering Raven during trance work, we decided that she was a group mascot. Her function seems to be to guide and protect. When I am in the seidh chair, Raven does not give me the answers, but if the visions are slow to come, I can ask her to lead me to a place where I can find them.

However, animals are not the only kinds of beings that may act as protectors, guides, or inspiration. Bari Mandelbaum says,

> When I travel the spirit worlds, I have a bear that usually accompanies me. When I am doing client work at the clinic, I usually am assisted by a fairy guide, who helps to keep *me* stable and protected,

and by one or more gods or Powers to help me find answers. Sometimes my ancestors may show up to help me find answers; sometimes a client's ancestors, guides, or guardians may show up as well. I worked with a Mormon woman once, and several beings calling themselves angels showed up as helpers for her, which was a framework she could relate to. I have even worked with Christian clients and have had Jesus show up for them as their helper and guide (though usually this will happen more in the context of guided imagery, where the client brings in Jesus rather than Him approaching me or showing up for me independently).

Caitlin Matthews, writing from England, reports a similar mix: "I have the ability to step into the shoes of any character that is helpful to my client and so often work through these ways. For myself, I also have those spirits—animals, ancestors, trees, gods, faeries, and other spirits who come depending upon the nature of the question."

The beings who become the companions of modern seers are part of the folklore of today's community, as are the power animals of a traditional shaman and the angelic, historical, and native spirit guides of the nineteenth-century spiritualist. Any or all of them may help us to find answers for others as well as for ourselves.

But What Are They Really?

One reason it is so important to be careful when working in spirit is that you do it with your soul. Here, above all, there is no such thing as a detached observer. When we finish our work, we cannot just put down our tools and walk away. The work of an oracle requires us to be open to other minds, and we cannot predict what emotional or psychic energies they will bring. One of the ways we can protect ourselves is by invoking inner guides. As with any other relationship, it is wise to learn as much as possible about the other party before letting him, her, or it into your heart.

The pythia at Delphi never questioned that a god was speaking through her, and the spirits the völva in Greenland dealt with were well known in her culture, but modern seers in search of an ally have a veritable smorgasbord of options. This became obvious when the spiritualist movement began to flourish, and a variety of spirits of varying degrees of wisdom appeared as their controls. An essay written by Herbert Thurston, S.J., in the 1930s summarizes the problem:

> Again, we know nothing about the nature or dispositions of the "spirits" who are supposed to be the agents of these phenomena. Certain records would even suggest that they may deliberately prompt some fraudulent device which results in the undoing of the medium. There is nothing to forbid our thinking that among them are evil spirits animated by a malicious purpose, though, on the other hand, some of the communicating intelligences appear truthful and kindly. . . .
>
> It is certainly curious that so large a proportion of those controls who seem somewhat more trustworthy than the rest profess to be Indians, calling themselves by such names as "Red Cloud," "White Feather," etc. There is not much likelihood that the beings who bore these names ever received baptism. But the fact is that we know nothing about the agencies who purport to communicate. The subconsciousness of the medium is no doubt responsible for by far the larger part of the messages received, but there is a residue which it is very hard to account for except as coming from some intelligence which is external to the world in which we live. (Thurston, 1995)

Each spiritual movement and tradition has its own "culture" and expectations that color how we perceive the information we receive. Spiritualism originated in the United States, and the cast list of controls has a distinctly American flavor. Once established, it is not surprising that as the movement spread, helping spirits appearing to new mediums took familiar forms.

In shamanic traditions, helping spirits are perceived as animal powers or ancestors, and in neo-shamanism, which models its practice on these cultures, it is the same. In the Classical world, it was assumed that oracular information came from the gods, whereas medieval Christians like Joan of Arc, belonging to a church that defined all non-Christian spirits as demonic, could identify helpful spirits only as saints or angels. Esoteric and New Age seers channel ascended masters or Tibetan adepts. Wiccans talk to ancestors, nature spirits, fairy folk, and gods, and Heathens talk to the gods, ancestors, and other wights of their mythology.

But no matter what they call themselves, the way inner allies function in various cultures is much the same. Does the fact that the shape seems to depend on the tradition rather than the other way around invalidate the spirit? Lorrie Wood offers an interesting perspective:

> I think that the shapes they use to talk to us are part of how they can talk to us in the first place from wherever they are. Or, to use some of the jargon I'd use at the office, the shape a spirit appears in is part of the protocol that the human and spirit negotiate between them when the relationship starts, as each communication flows, and from moment to moment as long as a connection is active.

But what do I mean by this?

Hosts on the Internet, starting with the computer in your home or office but including many, *many* other computers, like web and e-mail servers, communicate by protocols that are negotiated between them—not only in the instant of connection, but also moment by moment as the data flows through them. These protocols are published in public, where anyone might read them and put them to use in their own devices, so that *anyone* might connect to anyone else who has agreed to converse with one another in this way, whether they are using a dialup modem, an iPhone, or any other means.

This process starts with a request for communication. Every feature of that initial request—the language used, the medium that communicates with that language, and on and on—is there to explain what kind of machine is trying to make the connection, how fast it can speak and hear, whether it can speak and hear at the same time, and what kinds of things it can send and receive. This negotiation happens at computers' speed, in accordance with well-known, well-documented protocols, and when it's successful, not even professionals worry about it: It Just Works, and you're online and can read your e-mail, social media, and web pages.

The parallel between this and the nascent spirit worker's need to find *someone* to connect to should be obvious. The request, that naked *need*, if powered by sufficient focus and sincerity, is as hard to ignore as a ringing telephone. Eventually, *someone* will pick up—and everything about how that newbie has made that initial request for contact tells the spirit how to make the channel between them so that data can flow. As so much of our mental wiring is keyed to make life-or-death decisions based on rather scant data, the shape chosen has got to be one of the first things to get right.

As to what, or who, is on the other end of that line, the answers are many and not a one is conclusive. In the Otherworld, as on the Internet, nobody knows you're a dog.

If Lorrie is right, then the true nature of the powers that aid us is something that we embodied mortals cannot comprehend. What matters is not what they *are,* but what they *do.*

EARTH ENERGIES

In some lands, the prophets—Merlin or Moses, Thorbjorg or Fedelm—operated independently of any setting, but in the Mediterranean, the emphasis was on the oracular site and the deity who resided there. Although we know the names of a few of the men who served as priests at Delphi or thespodes at Claros, the prophets and pythias themselves remain anonymous. What mattered was the origin of wisdom, not the channel through which it was received.

The Greek writers also speculated on the sources of prophetic inspiration. Plutarch observes that

> the earth sends forth for men streams of many other potencies, some of them producing derangement, diseases, or deaths; others helpful, benignant, and beneficial, as is plain from the experience of persons who have come upon them. But the prophetic current and breath is most divine and holy, whether it issue by itself through the air or come in the company of running waters; for when it is instilled into the body, it creates in souls an unaccustomed and unusual temperament, the peculiarity of which it is hard to describe with exactness, but analogy offers many comparisons. (*De Defectu Oraculae* 40)

Other earth energies can also affect the result of a spae session. At midsummer of the year 2000, I attended a festival in Iceland sponsored by the Asatruarfelagið, the official Icelandic Heathen organization. The high point of the conference was a festival held at Thingvellir, at the meeting point between the European and North American tectonic plates. The two plates angle upward, and between them earth has filled the rift so that there is a grass-grown space varying between a dozen to thirty feet wide. The festival was not in the part of the park where the Icelandic Allthing was traditionally held, but farther along.

It had been my great ambition to do spae at Thingvellir, and at ten o'clock in the evening, we finally began. Although the sky was still light, the wind was growing cold, so we took shelter in one of the sinkholes in the flat area between the rift walls. There was no high seat, but I was able to perch on the slope. Usually I begin my process with a path working to the "Midgard that lies within" to make the psychological transition to a Norse cultural landscape. But when I am sitting in an inspiring natural location, I usually begin with my surroundings. In this case, it would have been hard to imagine a more culturally appropriate setting, and I found myself journeying straight down from where I was sitting and rather unexpectedly ended up in a rocky chamber that in shape was the mirror image of the place where I sat. There seemed no need to go any further.

Just before the festival, Iceland had experienced two strong earthquakes, and since they often seemed to come in threes, I was not surprised that the first question was whether there would soon be another one. I opened my awareness to seek an answer. "Twitch . . . twitch. . . ." It was hard not to laugh. I was sitting on one of the earth's great fault lines, and I could sense a little tremor as soon as I heard the question. In a moment, there was another one. The entire island, one of the most geologically active places on earth, was twitching constantly. It took some strength of will to narrow my search to the tension that would signal another large quake on the way. But I could find none and reported that there would be no more major tremors for some time, which proved to be true.

The problem was that sitting in that place, the earth energies were so strong that when people began to ask other questions, all I wanted to do was to explore this wonderful world the landspirits were showing me, and I had great difficulty in seeing anything relevant to humans at all.

THE WORLDS WITHIN

In my survey of contemporary seers, I asked where they looked for answers. Sometimes, as we have seen, the answer comes directly, but at others it is necessary to journey. Most of the seers reported getting information in a variety of ways, depending on the question. Those working in the northern tradition operate mostly within traditional Germanic spiritual geography, using the Worldtree and the Nine Worlds as an internal map of the Otherworld. They may journey to the Well of Urð or to Helheim (in Heathen tradition, the general home of the ancestors, not a place of punishment), especially when the querent wants to talk to an ancestor. In the lore, Odin goes to Hlithskjalf, his Seat of Seeing, when he wants to know what is going on in the world, but our experience has been that it only shows what is going on in the present, and these days we humans find it easier to get that kind of information from the Internet. The Well of Mimir holds a great store of data, but very few have the gift to download it, much less interpret what it means.

One place with a clear relationship to fate is the Well of Urð/Wyrd, where the three Norns lay down *ørlög*, a term meaning something like primal law, the layers of effects resulting from previous choices and actions that shape what is to come. The names of the Norns come from forms of two verbs meaning "to be." Urð deals with what has been, Verdandi with what is becoming, and Skuld with what "should" result. The seer may look into the well as into a scrying mirror, or connect with the web of wyrd. As Rod Landreth puts it,

> I feel that I am looking directly at the ørlög of the person and all the wyrd attached to that person. Then I look into what I can only call "Skuld's realm," at the possible and probable lines that come from the "Verdhandi realm" of the now. The most probable line based upon the querent's question sort of highlights or "bolds" itself and I "go into" that thread of wyrd. At that point, I am merely relating what I see as the most probable event that I *see* in front of me, rather like describing a movie to a blind person.

There is no single location in which all questions can be answered and no single source of answers. When we need to speak to a particular power, we often have to journey to a more appropriate location. To do this requires familiarity with the inner map of the Nine Worlds and the mental discipline to find one's way out and back again.

One of our most memorable examples of this has become known in Seidhjallr as "Jennifer Goes to Mars." At one of our smaller, local presentations, a gentleman said that he had been looking at images of the "face on Mars" and wanted to know if there was life there. The seeress's first response was that she could not answer that question here. I motioned to the questioner to wait, as it was clear that she was journeying. Presently she answered, "Of course, there are wights [the Norse word for spirits] on the red planet, but as for the kind of life you mean, no, I am sorry to say that there are no physical beings on Mars." There was another slight pause. Then she said, "I have to go now. I have no more air." She had apparently constructed for herself an astral air bubble in order to travel to outer space, as opposed to inner space. Some time later, I saw a film of footage taken by the Mars Lander, and there were the Mars wights, in the form of dust devils whirling madly across the sandy plain.

Those who work in a pan-pagan context range more widely, often journeying to a generic Otherworld from which they can access specific cultural locations. Nanette Boyster, who comes from a family with a tradition of seership, has developed her own process:

> I go to three different places: the Void, where I can find dead people easily (my friend Lisa refers to this as the gap where everything began), the lands of the Fae (different isles where I can find different Celtic groups and also a good place to access landspirits), and Asgard. I don't go walking or whatever; I just picture where I want to be and "shift" to it. I've been to these places so many times I don't need to follow the "paths" anymore, and frankly, I get bored when I have to slow down enough to walk others there. Also, I can "call up" mist that I can use to transfer me around, if needed.

Seers may also answer questions from a neutral visionary state, characterized as the "universal web," the "deep collective universal wisdom," or "thin air." In Part Two, we will explore the use of journeying and imagery in reaching a state in which one can access information.

VI

MANIA AND MANTIKE: ISSUES AND OPPORTUNITIES

> For prophecy is a madness, and the prophetess at Delphi and the priestesses at Dodona when out of their senses have conferred great benefits on Hellas, both in public and private life, but when in their senses few or none.
>
> Plato, *Phaedrus*

That oracles can "confer great benefits" we know from the reports of those who have asked questions. But can there be hazards in hearing a prophecy—or giving one?

SHRIEKING SIBYLS, DELPHIC DEMENTIA

In Virgil's *Aeneid* VI, we are given a harrowing picture of the Sibyl's trance:

> *Just as the Trojans reached the threshold,*
> *the virgin cried—"Now call upon the Fates*
> *for oracles! The god is here! The god!"*
> *As she says this before the doors, her face*
> *and color alter suddenly; her hair*
> *is disarrayed; her breast heaves, and her wild*
> *heart swells with frenzy; she is taller now;*
> *her voice is more than human, for the power*
> *of the god is closing in; he breathes upon her. . . .*
> *she rages, savage, in her cavern, tries*
> *to drive the great god from her breast. So much*
> *the more, he tires out her raving mouth;*
> *he tames her wild heart, shapes by crushing force.*

The image is dramatic and has certainly contributed to a tradition of the female oracular performance as a wild-eyed frenzy. Dempsey comments that the female oracles are especially prone to orgiastic religious seizure (1918, 55). However, he then goes on to note Plutarch's evidence that the pythia was required to be a well-balanced person and underwent her period of retreat and purification so that she would come to her task calm and undisturbed. He only reports one case of hysteria, when the omens taken before the oracle were negative, but the ceremony went ahead anyway: "[A]t her first responses it was at once plain from the harshness of her voice that she was not responding properly; she was like a labouring ship and was filled with a mighty and baleful spirit. Finally she became hysterical and with a frightful shriek rushed towards the exit and threw herself down" (*De Defectu Oraculae* 51).

Despite the stereotype, the ideal person to serve as a seer was the opposite of a madman. As Iamblichus comments,

> For in what does the enthusiastic inspiration resemble melancholy or drunkenness or any other form of alienation originating from morbid conditions of the body? What oracle can ever be produced from distempers of the body? Is not a product of such a kind wholly a destruction, but divine possession a perfecting and deliverance of the soul? Does not the worthless trance happen at the same time with debility, but the superior enthusiastic rapture with complete reign? In short, to speak plainly, the latter, being in a tranquil condition as relates to its own life and intelligence, gives itself to be used by another; but the former, operating with its peculiar species, renders them utterly wicked and turbulent. (*De Mysteriis* 3:7)

SOUND MINDS AND SOUND ANSWERS

Is prophecy, as Plato tells us, a madness? Or by this does he mean an altered state of consciousness? The literature on prophets and oracles suggests that, far from being "mad," in their ordinary lives, they are among the more sensible and well-balanced members of the community. The priestesses at Delphi were ordinary women of good families, and the priests at Claros were respectable men who returned to their businesses after their term as oracle. A Celtic filidh had to survive twenty years of rigorous training. The völvas of the far North had to keep themselves and their students safe while traveling around a politically and climatically challenging countryside.

It is both my opinion and my experience that whether the imbalance is permanent or temporary, no one who is not in good mental health should be allowed to work as a seer. In a practice that requires us to detach as much of our consciousness as possible not only from personal feelings, but also from awareness of the outside world, we must be able to rise above our own concerns. To receive and transmit answers clearly, we must understand our own prejudices, preconceptions, and vulnerabilities. No matter how hard we try, the information we receive is going to be filtered through minds formed by our culture and experiences. We owe it to the questioners to make that filter as free of distortion as possible.

Seers also need to be healthy for their own sake. Doing oracle work requires physical endurance and the mental stability to withstand the emotional impact of other minds. A vulnerable seer can be devastated by contact with someone whose problems have an unhealthy dynamic with his or her own. Training involves constant self-examination. Until we know our own demons, we cannot tell the difference between what is coming through, or to, the questioner and what is our own.

HAZARDS OF THE TRADE

When we do weekend workshops, there is a point on Sunday, when the participants are still feeling euphoric about their trance work the night before, when we ask them to think about what kinds of psychological hazards and ethical issues might be involved in serving as an oracle. In over twenty years of practice, we have never lost a seeress, but when we deliberately close the door on consensus reality and lower the barriers that protect our psyches, the potential for problems is always there. Even when the oracle does not set out to deceive, history and literature are full of stories like that of Macbeth, in which a questioner comes to grief through misunderstanding his answer. So what are the issues involved in oracular practice? What are the dangers to seer and questioner? And how can those dangers be avoided?

In the Darkover books, Marion Zimmer Bradley was fond of saying that an untrained telepath was a danger to herself and others. Certainly a mentally unhealthy seer could potentially endanger herself and the questioners. Without a strong ego, she might not be able to distinguish her own reality from that of the person asking the question. Without balance and control, she might project her own needs and fears onto the vision or blast her own traumas into the minds linked to hers by the ritual.

To avoid potential problems, we ask those who are interested in oracular practice to work with us in other groups for a year or more before we admit them to Seidhjallr, and to work with the team for a while before we put them into the high seat at a festival.

Those who wish to train for oracular practice should consider the questions at the beginning of Part Two carefully, and work through the exercises in *Trance-Portation*, paying particular attention to the "Check-sums" process in Chapter Four. The most powerful answers come from those questions that are motivated by the greatest need. If you are going to open yourself up to other people's traumas, you need to first identify and deal with your own.

Even those whom we judge to be well balanced must be in a healthy emotional state at the time of the ritual. The ancients also recognized that sometimes everyone has a bad day, as when Plutarch observes, "It is better that she should not go there and surrender herself to the control of the god, when she is not completely unhampered (as if she were a musical instrument, well strung and well tuned), but is in a state of emotion and instability" (*De Defectu Oraculae* 50).

Even if you cannot spend three days in prayer and fasting before working, it is essential to detach yourself from the concerns of ordinary life. Shortly before one of our sessions, one of the women who was scheduled to serve as a seeress came to tell me that she had just had a fight with her boyfriend. She was in tears, and it was obvious to both of us that she was not going to be able to calm down in time. Although this put more stress on the two seeresses who remained, we were grateful for her honesty.

At Delphi, the failure of the sacrificial goat to tremble when sprinkled with water was an omen that the oracular session would fail. Most modern seers and diviners do not take omens, nor are the outcomes usually disastrous, but there can be problems. Fortunately, most of them can be dealt with through training or with support from others.

One of the most common problems is running out of steam. Psychic work is still labor, and an oracular session can be exhausting on the physical as well as the spiritual level. Seers may complain of cold after a session and are almost always hungry, so we make food available for the team after the ritual. In my own experience, that empty feeling in the pit of my stomach is the signal that it's time to quit. The greatest number of questions I ever answered in one session was fifty-one, at a Starwood festival some years ago. I knew I was running out of juice when my stomach began to growl. Afterward, I devoured the largest steak I could find.

One advantage of working with a team at a large festival is that another seer can take over when the first one tires. At the same time, trance work can produce a rush that makes it hard to sleep. The seer should take special care in grounding if this becomes a problem. Vigorous physical exercise may also help to balance the energies.

A more subtle problem is the drain on psychic energy. Connecting with one questioner after another can be exhausting. Jordsvin has reported "getting sick from a big public Seidhr session where people were leaving as they got their answers. Felt like I was running off a battery that was running down." He said he resolved the problem by telling folks that they needed to stay and support him in exchange for having him journey/see/ask questions and relay answers for them.

Having a larger number of people in the ritual can also be helpful. One of the things we can learn from traditional shamanic practice is that spiritual work should be an interactive process. The energy that the shaman uses to work for the patient is raised by the community. In an oracular session, if the other participants agree, the seer can draw energy from them. One way to do this is by having the group chant or sing.

Another possible hazard is the fact that once you are in trance, you may not want to leave. The solution to this problem is the discipline that results from practice and a conditioned response to cues for returning to consensus reality. These should be internalized, but support can be provided by a partner or team. Some people find it hard to close down once they have opened up to others and will continue to pick up information after the session even when no question has been asked.

For most of these problems, the solution is to review and practice your skills in grounding. You will find some basic techniques in the first part of *Trance-Portation*. Other options include physical stimuli, such as drinking water or tasting some strong flavor, such as salt or citric acid. Eating a protein-rich meal will also help. In general, anything that intensifies your connection to your physical body will help you to deal with the aftereffects of trance.

Spending a lot of time in the spirit world can bring you to the attention of those who live there. As Bari Mandelbaum puts it, "All of a sudden you're 'on the map' and at greater risk of having random spirits, gods, and other non-corporeals following you home. Sometimes this is great, and sometimes it's a distraction."

Some problems come from the questioners or the questions. These may be in the form of more information than you really need to answer the question, much less want to know. Or you may end up sharing someone's trauma. Some years ago, the children of a member of our community died in a fire. Everyone was in shock, and not too surprisingly, somebody asked Jordsvin a question about it. "I saw a bunch of fires in Hel," he remembers. "I knew I'd freak if I saw any burned babies." He resolved the problem by telling his guide, "Winifred, get me the hell out of here!"

The seer must be able to recognize when a vision will be unbearable and extract himself or ask help from an inner or outer guide. This, like a question that hits one of the seer's own sore spots, is one of the situations in which he should recuse himself from answering and refuse the question or pass it on to another seer.

Most questioners have the manners to keep silent until well after the session if they are not happy with their answer. But one seer remembers being accosted by a questioner while still tired and vulnerable immediately after a session. The questioner accused him of giving his own opinion instead of that of the god he was channeling. The seer responded by revising his process to make it clear to everyone that he could not know who had asked questions.

Galina Krasskova says,

> The biggest problem I've had is that people often come to a diviner or oracle wanting to hear confirmation that what they *want* is going to happen. They don't want the truth. They don't want to delve into their wyrd. They want their own expectations and hopes to be validated, and it doesn't work that way.
>
> I've also often had to deliver unpleasant information. No one likes to hear that. Sometimes I've had clients get very defensive (particularly when a Dis [female ancestor] or even a deity was being very insistent

through me that the client take responsibility for the mess he or she was currently in). Sometimes people project their own anger and defensiveness onto me. That's never pleasant. I'm aware that it can happen, and when I'm in oracular headspace, I can usually see it coming a mile away, and I know it's not really about me. It's just a hazard of the work.

Bias on the part of the seer is always a potential issue. Try as we will for clarity, our perceptions and responses will still be affected by our background and experiences. I always remind participants that the answer is coming through two filters, that of the seer and their own, and what a word or image means to one person and to another may not be the same. If the answer seems dire or confusing, they should get a second opinion, but in the end, what they do with the information is their own responsibility.

The ideal is to find a middle ground, neither allowing ourselves to feel devastated when we can get nothing or get it wrong, nor thinking we are goddesses when we get something right. Patricia Lafayllve says, "We have to be aware of and avoid what I call the 'grand high poobah' effect, too—when we surround ourselves with people who compliment us on our abilities and we lose track of what our abilities actually *are,* where we begin and end, and we kind of start believing our own hype."

We must never forget that we are taking a great responsibility. Patricia also points out,

> Whenever a person asks a question and we give an answer, what we've done, in effect, alters their wyrd. Let's say, for instance, the person asks, "Should I take path A or B?" I answer by describing the pros and cons of both, but then also mention a path C that they haven't seen. Whichever path the querent ends up choosing, they're making that choice based at least in part in my answers—that's wyrd in action. I may just have altered the most likely outcome their life should have taken. It seems like a small thing, answering a simple question like that, but there are ramifications to everything we do, and we often don't see them all, nor are we in a place where we'll ever find out.

And yet unless we take that responsibility, we cannot help. We cannot guarantee that what we say will be *the* truth, much less that the questioner will understand and use it. All we can do is to offer ourselves as channels through which truth can flow.

We also warn participants against following the seer into the deeper trance state in which he or she answers questions. If the ritual includes a path working, the image of a barrier, such as the gate to Helheim, makes it easier to distinguish between states of consciousness. This is not likely to be a problem when the session is one-on-one, but a large public ritual raises a lot of energy, which can carry participants as well as the seer along. In an audience of pagans, furthermore, there will be a number of people who have done enough trance work themselves to be attracted to the oracular state and who are certain that they have the skill to handle it. Sensing that another person has come along for the ride can be distracting to the seer and certainly takes more energy from the seer and the rest of the team, who are responsible for delivering everyone back to ordinary reality at the end of the ceremony.

Channeling deities can also sometimes be a problem for the seer. If the need of the questioner is enough to invoke the presence of the deity, a seer who is open may end up possessed regardless of whether or not he is willing to work with that deity in that way. In two such cases that I know of, it was Odin who came through. Another seer has had problems with Freyja dropping in unexpectedly. When this happens, the questioner may get a good answer, but the seer feels violated. This problem is a topic for another book. Suffice it to say that dealing with nonconsensual possession requires negotiation, discipline, and the assistance of a guide who has been informed about the agreements between the seer and the spirits and who can act to control or banish any being that breaks them.

We should also consider the possible hazards to the questioners. Bari Mandelbaum cautions,

> Don't ask a question unless you really want to know the answer! You run the hazard of getting more information than you can handle. When you ask a question, you put yourself on the spirit world map potentially, so to speak . . ., which is either a good thing or a bad thing, depending on your perspective. I got nabbed by Odin at a Seidh ritual when I was a questioner. (It was not what I was expecting to have happen, to say the least! I don't regret it now, but it sure was a huge big deal when it first happened, and completely and irrevocably changed

the course of my life.) There can also be the danger of becoming dependent on seers for making your choices for you.

Dan Campbell also has something to say about connecting with spirits:

> I've generally found it wise for practitioners to ally themselves with spirits they are sure they can trust, if only to keep other spirits at a distance (and so less bothersome, if not outright harmful). If the local wights are honored appropriately, and the warders remain aware of querents' emotional/spiritual states, then the risk to the querent should be minimal, as the oracular practitioner is the one doing the spiritual/magical work. But one does have to take care, as a seer, how one facilitates the relationship between the querent and any spirits that may be providing or involved in the answers to their question. A querent could weaken, strengthen, establish, or end such a relationship in the course of asking their question and receiving an answer, and seers would do well to recognize when that is or could be happening and to help the querent to a good outcome.

Just as we work with the seers after a ritual to make sure they have grounded and detached from the spirit world, we try to do the same for the other participants, encouraging them to consult us if they have any problems or unusual reactions or experiences.

TRUTH OR CONSEQUENCES?

Each time I sit in the seidhjallr, there comes a moment when I wonder if the magic will work or whether this time the answers will fail. On the whole, I think this is a healthy anxiety, a corrective to overconfidence. Even at Delphi, they waited for confirmation from the god before going ahead with the ritual, and the Greenland völva required the cooperation of the spirits in order to give answers.

When the moment of truth comes for me, I can only offer myself as a channel through which wisdom can flow. If nothing seems to be happening, I call on Raven to lead me to a vision, and so far, an answer has always appeared. But sometimes the right answer may be no answer. We strive to open the way for the truth to come through, but what does the seer do when what she sees is too terrible to say? Patricia Lafayllve expresses the problem in this way:

> Probably the most common problem, for me, materializes in one of two ways. Either I get no answer at all—nothing whatsoever—or, occasionally, I'll get answers and then hear something to the effect of "But don't tell him that." It's a moral dilemma. The first is the easiest—I believe it's a moral imperative for me to be as honest as I can, and if I can't answer a person's question, I say so. I don't try to fish or use my own insight—I just tell them that I am sorry, but I have nothing for them. It makes me sad because I want to help, and sometimes I can tell that the questioner really needs the answer. . . . But if I don't get one, I can't ethically give one. So I don't.
>
> The other is more complicated—the answer is right there, but I am being told confidential information. As a seidhkona and gythja [priestess], I believe that confidential information needs to be kept that way—even if it's coming from a long-dead grandmother. So I will do a mental rephrasing and ask . . . well, then, what *can* I tell them? That often works—what ends up happening is I have a fuller picture and can then give the answer the questioner needs in the moment. It's an ethical thing, again, but I think part of being a seidhkona, gythja, or other type of spiritual leader is recognizing that not everyone is ready to hear what you have to say. There's a balancing act involved, and it's a struggle every time to find that balance between what you know and what you should say.
>
> As another example, if someone asks a question related to their health, I always tell them that I am not a physician and all I can do is give a spirit-answer. Maybe I see a blockage in the person's energy flow—that doesn't mean it's a malignant tumor, necessarily, but on the other hand, it is up to a trained, licensed, medical professional to deal with any physical issues. It's that "specialty" answer all over again—go to the specialist best able to get you the information you need to have.

The physician's oath says "Do no harm," but the contract between the seer and the source is to transmit the message as clearly as you can. The "second stage" trance in which the seer gives answers is by definition a state of extreme passivity. For me, that state is like being in a sensory-deprivation tank. I float in the warm darkness, needing nothing, desiring nothing. When the question comes, it is at first an intrusion, and it is hard to summon the will to look for an answer. At this point I may ask Raven to help me find an image. As I begin to describe it, the vision clarifies, until I can not only describe it fully but often interpret it as well.

The seer's obligation is not only to recognize and avoid being influenced by his biases, but also, in theory, to reach a state in which he has no opinion and can transmit what he perceives with the same dispassion as a court reporter recording what she hears. But as Patricia Lafayllve points out, it doesn't always work that way. Sometimes the question elicits an overwhelming sense of yes or no. Other questions trigger a download of information, which the seer relays. And still others stimulate visions.

Whatever form the response takes, there might be a number of reasons not to tell "the truth, the whole truth, and nothing but the truth." First, as in Patricia's example, whatever power is providing the information may forbid full disclosure. Second, the information may be extremely sensitive. This is not a problem in a one-on-one session, but when the question is asked in a large public ritual, the seer may need to call the questioner up and whisper it into his ear. Caitlin Matthews comments,

> For the questioner in a public session, however intimate the group, the answers can be exposing, though I also feel that the humility and leveling of such sessions is a great corrective to our "eternally right and perfect" persona! For the seer, the oracle comes or not from sources beyond their control—what is seen or understood by the mediator has to sometimes be given in terms that can be received. Sometimes we see something very difficult for the client, like a cloud over them or an actual event. Sometimes we are aware of things done or said, and we must not judge.

Another option is to clothe the answer in imagery that only the questioner will understand. This can be especially important when the question is about health. When the answer comes in images, not only is its meaning often hidden from the rest of the participants, but it may be incomprehensible to the seer as well.

The safest response when vision shows a possible problem is to refer the matter to an appropriate professional. At one session, a woman asked when she would get pregnant. The seeress saw a dark mass in the woman's uterus. Not wanting to announce this in a public ritual, she answered that there would be difficulties and urged the questioner to consult a physician as soon as possible.

The style in which an answer is delivered may also affect the way in which it is received, if not the validity of its content. The appropriate mode for oracular answers seems to depend on the context. Those who consulted the Delphic oracle expected responses in the style of Apollo. At some periods, replies were translated into verse. The Viking Age spákonas, on the other hand, appear to have given straightforward answers. Modern psychics also speak in a conversational style, while the ascended masters channeled by New Age mystics employ an elevated and sometimes archaic mode. Our own seers have personal styles that vary in formality, which can cause a problem if a questioner who assumes that an oracle will speak in an archaic manner gets an answer in modern slang. Some seers develop an "oracular persona," with a name that is used only in spiritual work, and shift to an appropriate style of communication when it is used.

REWARDS

Given the potential for problems, why do we continue to do the job? Over and over again, the seers who responded to the questionnaire spoke of their call—or perhaps compulsion—to serve. Especially for people whose sensitivity may have caused them trouble in the past, the opportunity to put it to use is a relief and a validation. We are grateful to be of use to others. When a seer works within a close community, there may be additional benefits. Dan Campbell says,

> Something I have noticed, both at Hasaeti's spae sessions and at the oracular seidhr sessions at Trothmoot, is that spae can be understood as the community talking to its unconscious. There is a tendency for "time-honored truths," even if clichés, to come up as answers—and for "time-honored anxieties" to appear as questions. The dialogue that happens during spae often sounds like an individual seeking affirmation/support from the culture of their community, and that culture, through the seer, providing that reassurance/clarification. I've also noticed that querents who have something in common with the oracular practitioners—whether

friendship, similar religious beliefs, or common life background— are more likely to understand and find meaning in the answers they receive. Several times, I've seen a question asked by a querent not otherwise known by others in the gathered group who received the answer with bafflement while there were small affirmative nods or other "I agree" body language from the gathered group, and then several attempts by the seer to bridge the gap.

Bari Mandelbaum says,

> I think it's an incredible benefit to the community to have people/ rituals they can go to in order to get help, relief, confirmation, and guidance and to connect with the sacred. Not everyone can or wants to connect with the spirit world in these ways, so it is very useful to have individuals and groups providing this service. I think oracle work benefits the whole community's connection to the Powers as well. It's somewhat easier, I think, to believe in a god or goddess with whom you can actually talk on occasion or receive messages and guidance.

But there are many ways to help others and more reasons than service to do the work of a seer. In oracular trance, we move in a wider world. Given the excuse of the questioner's need, we have a reason to seek places and beings we would not otherwise try to contact. We feel the questioner's passion as well as his pain; we see through his eyes, understand concepts, share experiences we would not otherwise know. In a sacred exchange of energies, we offer ourselves to serve the community and the gods. When a god appears to answer a question, we feel the questioner's wonder and the love with which the deity responds.

Winifred Hodge Rose says,

> I love this work more than almost anything else. I get to share in experiences with the deities by helping them and the querent com- municate, and I love that. . . . Every person is a world in oneself, deep, wide and mysterious, and it is an honor and a wonder to touch on these worlds through spaecraft service. My experience of the Worlds is so much wider than one person's normally could be because of this. It is so very interesting to watch and wonder how spaecraft works, to form hypotheses and then get lucky when a situation comes up that can test them.

VII

THE PROBLEM OF PROPHECY

Croesus: Is Apollo not ashamed of having encouraged Croesus with his oracles to make war on the Persians in the belief that he would destroy Cyrus' power, from which enterprise he shall have Croesus' chains as first-fruits? And is it the custom of Hellenic gods to be unthankful?

Pythia: Not even deity can escape destiny. Croesus has expiated a misdeed of his ancestor five generations back, who serving a woman's guile, killed his lord and took a throne that was not his. Although Apollo wanted the fall of Sardis to happen under Croesus' sons and not in Croesus' reign, he could not persuade the Moirai; the best that he could do was to persuade them to postpone the fall of Sardis for three years. Then Apollo saved Croesus from burning. Croesus does not rightly blame the Oracle. When Apollo predicted that if Croesus made war on the Persians he would destroy a great realm he should have sent to ask whether Apollo meant Cyrus' realm or his own. Since Croesus did not understand the response properly, he must blame himself.

Quasi-historical Delphic answer 103,
identified by Fontenrose as not genuine (1978, 303)

I began my exploration of oracular practice in 1989 with certain assumptions. One was the idea that, as with greatness, some could achieve the ability to serve as oracles as well as being born seers or having the power thrust upon them. Another was that oracles do useful work for the community. A third was that an oracle is the same thing as a prediction. The first two beliefs have been generally confirmed by my experience, but as time goes on I have become increasingly dubious regarding the third, and that, in turn, has caused me to question the assumptions underlying oracular practice.

The oracle quoted above is the last in a series of questions attributed to King Croesus of Lydia. It seems to be an attempt to clear Apollo of the charge of being either deliberately misleading or just plain wrong. But the Delphic oracle is not the only one to have sometimes confused its clients. As Howard Dobin observes, "The history of prophecy is the history of infinite interpretation. That legacy of prophetic disappointment and misinterpretation attests to the unlimited license of symbolic meaning—exposing prophecy as the epitome of nonrepresentational language, rather than the authentic, divine model of referential meaning" (Dobin 1990, 25).

PERILOUS PROPHECIES

Oracular answers, especially when cast in poetic or allusive form, have the simultaneous advantage and disadvantage of being open to multiple interpretations. "Merlinic" prophecy was always political, promising the return of legendary leaders and expressing hopes of a suppressed people. Every few years, today's tabloids publish the prophecies of Nostradamus, reinterpreted to meet current needs.

The Question of Croesus

Whether the oracles given to King Croesus are authentic or folkore, they demonstrate not only the iconic status of the Delphic oracle in the Greek world, but also the strengths and limitations of oracular prediction. As the story goes, King Croesus, having built Lydia into a great kingdom, was considering whether he should attack Persia and make it greater still. He tested the oracles with a question about his actions on a given day. When the pythia at Delphi answered correctly, he sent again, with the question, "Should I make war on the Persians? And with what army should I ally myself?" The answer was, "If you march against the Persians [if you cross the river Halys (verse form)], you will destroy a great kingdom. Find the strongest Hellenes and ally yourself with them" (Herodotus, in Fontenrose 1978, 302). The king took this to mean that he would conquer. He crossed the river and was defeated. The kingdom he destroyed was his own. We see how the oracle replied when he complained about his answer in the quote with which this chapter began.

The Trouble with Tiresias

One of the problems with prophecy, especially in fiction, is the unfortunate truth that sometimes it's what you do know that hurts you. Consider the case of Tiresias in Sophocles' *Oedipus Rex*. When the oracle at Delphi tells the Thebans that the city's troubles are due to the unavenged murder of the former king, the new king Oedipus demands that Tiresias, "the god-inspired seer in whom above all other men is truth inborn," help him find the killer. Only when Oedipus accuses him of having had a hand in the murder himself does Tiresias reply, "I charge thee to abide by thine own proclamation; from this day speak not to these or me. Thou art the man, thou the accursed polluter of this land."

The story is an illustration of the perils of prophecy. A generation earlier, Delphi had prophesied that the son of King Laius would kill his father. The king ordered the boy to be exposed, but the child was rescued. Then Oedipus himself left the parents who adopted him because he learned he was destined to kill his father; thus, he found himself at the crossroads where he met the king, his true father, and did kill him. The tragic irony is that both their efforts to avoid fate brought it to pass.

As Fontenrose points out, although unambiguous prophecies, such as the prediction that it would take ten years for the Greeks to conquer Troy, are common in the legendary responses attributed to the oracle at Delphi, of the seventy-four historical responses he collected, only two make clear predictions. To a question on whether the Spartans should make war on Athens, the oracle answered, "If they fight with all their strength, victory will be theirs; and Apollo himself will assist them, invited or uninvited" (Historical Answer 5). Clearly Delphi approved this war, which started after the Athenians had broken a truce, but the conditional format allows for other factors to change the outcome.

When the Oracle Was Wrong

Not too surprisingly, the threat of invasion by King Cyrus of Persia sent the Athenians off to Delphi to ask the advice of the god. The answer must have been a shock: "Do not stay; fly to the ends of the earth, leaving your houses and city. For the whole body is unsound; nothing is left.

Fire and war destroy it" (Quasi-historical Answer 146). But as we know, Cyrus was defeated, and Athens survived. Despite the reputation of the oracle, there were some who doubted. In Euripides' play *Ion*, the oracles regarding a son for King Xuthus contradict the evidence. As the boy Ion protests, "The god is true, or prophecy is in vain—this troubles my heart, mother, and with reason" (*Ion* 1536). We too should consider well what kind of truth oracles can give us, and how we should use it.

ON THE FAILURE (OR SUCCESS) OF ORACLES

A reader who is committed to the possibilities of oracle work encounters Plutarch's essay *De Defectu Oraculae*—translated as "On the Failure of Oracles" or "On the Decline of Oracles"—with some alarm. If Plutarch, who was himself a priest at Delphi, doubted, is the entire tradition a delusion?

When one reads the essay, however, it becomes clear that Plutarch is not questioning the Oracle's veracity, but its popularity. Things always look rosier in retrospect, and compared to the oracles of legend, activity at Delphi had certainly diminished by Plutarch's day, although the oracle enjoyed a significant revival shortly thereafter and continued in operation until it was shut down by Theodosius I in 395 CE. Nonetheless, the student of oracular practice cannot contemplate that title without a shiver of doubt. Are oracles really *true?* Can they predict the future, or are we all self-deluded seekers of thrills, or worse, power? And if the oracle does get it right, is that the result of divine inspiration or fraud?

Skeptics start from an assumption that seers cannot possibly be getting their information by supernatural means. They have come up with a variety of sometimes very creative explanations for where they do get their answers. Debunkers of spiritualism and of TV psychics like John Edwards point out that before a séance, the psychics and mediums gather data about and from their clients from which to deduce information, and then they ask leading questions to develop it. Debunkers of the Greek oracles have proposed that even though the seer was kept in seclusion, the priests who staffed the oracle had plenty of opportunity to pick up clues as they prepared the questioners, and they could fine-tune whatever the seer mumbled to fit the questions when they polished his or her answers afterward. An even more inventive theory proposed by Robert

Temple suggests that the Delphic priests maintained an information-gathering system throughout the Mediterranean world and used carrier pigeons to send the news.

During the past twenty years, I have participated in scores of oracular sessions as a seer or member of the supporting staff and heard hundreds of answers, which gives me a database that, if not objective, is at least extensive. My conclusion, based on observation and shaped by my understanding of Germanic cosmology, is that the best an oracle can do is to discern what *is*.

Let us reconsider the story of King Croesus. The question and answer at the beginning of this chapter are the last in a series recorded in the first book of Herodotus' *Histories*. To test the oracles, Croesus had asked the oracle to say what he was doing on a certain day. It was an unlikely action—boiling the meat of a lamb and a turtle in a bronze cauldron. Receiving a correct answer from Delphi, the king sent men to ask his real question. Croesus took the answer to mean that he would win, but as we have seen, it was his own empire, not that of Cyrus, that fell. What are we to conclude? Was this a deliberately ambiguous oracle of the sort that will bring credit to the prophet however things turn out, since you can always say that the questioner misinterpreted the answer? Do oracles, like Tolkien's elves, "say both no and yes?"

I offer another interpretation, which is that the pythia told as much truth as she could see *at that time*. She could answer the first question clearly because the action it involved was taking place in real time. But the result of a war between Lydia and Persia depended on factors that could not be known until the battle itself. If the two empires had not been closely matched in power, Croesus would not have needed to ask about the outcome. Thus, all the pythia could see was a conditional truth—if they fought, one would lose.

How then can we account for *unambiguous* forecasts? The literature of prophecy certainly includes many such examples, and we sometimes hear from contemporary questioners that predictions have been fulfilled. Did those seers simply make a lucky guess?

My opinion is that Cyrus and Croesus had an equal potential for victory, and so no clear probability could be discerned. In other situations, the forces favoring one course of action may be so strong that the outcome is perceived as a certainty. It is also true, of course, that believers, like those who questioned the pythia and who attend our oracular sessions today, are predisposed to remember events that reinforce their belief and discount or explain away those that do not.

Unfortunately, to take exit polls after spae sessions would detract from the experience, so aside from the occasional questioner who gets up muttering that the answer was *wrong* (usually when it was advisory, not predictive), the only ones we hear from are people who were happy with their answers. The answers recorded in ancient times were even more likely to be those that had been confirmed. I therefore have no figures on the percentage of correct answers given by seers, but after participating in oracular sessions as seer or support staff for so many years, I can offer a hypothesis.

As you can see from the analysis of question types given in Chapter IV, many questions do not require foreknowledge. People want guidance on what they can or should do to live better lives. The seer may not be able to see *the* future, but he or she often seems to get information and images from the unconscious of the questioner, and is able to articulate and interpret feelings and needs of which the person asking the question was not consciously aware. If the question itself does not involve a choice, it is still likely to depend on probabilities, and a seer who is tuned in to the currents of the universe will be able to discern how they may interact. When a question specifically does involve the future, we often find an answer that lays out choices rather than certainties.

Matthew, the proprietor of Mysteries, a psychic center in London, believes that "the future hasn't happened yet. All that psychics and mediums are doing is tapping into something that is already known." He believes that "the universe is integrated and that there's some kind of collective consciousness. Psychics use this like a mystical grapevine, listening in to our past and our present and giving suggestions about our futures" (Little 2009, 7).

In his analysis of concepts of world and time in early Germanic culture, Paul C. Bauschatz points out, "There are no explicit references in early Germanic materials to a concept like the future. Events that seem to us to be future-oriented turn out, when carefully examined, to refer directly to the interaction of the past with events of the nonpast, of that which has occurred with that which is in the process of occurring" (Bauschatz 1982, 141). The present is created by the events that have taken place and the choices that have been made in the past. The "future," therefore, cannot be fixed because it is eternally coming into being.

I prefer to believe that the future is not fated, but flexible. The waters of the Well of Wyrd are always in motion, some currents weak and some strong, but all of them eternally swirling. There is always hope. There is always choice. There is always the work of will.

PREDICTION AND PROBABILITY

If oracles do not predict *the* future, then what *do* they do?

The first attempt to scientifically study psychic phenomena began during the nineteenth century, when spiritualism swept Europe and America, just as New Age beliefs did a century later. The British Society for Psychical Research was set up in 1882 to scientifically investigate paranormal and psychic claims. One of its most important subjects was a woman called Leonora Piper. She practiced no deception, and yet she was consistently able to provide correct details and information about people she had never met before. After exhaustive study, William James concluded that while in trance, she could access information that she could not possibly have acquired in her waking state.

Mrs. Piper worked with several spirit guides, some of whom were historical figures. However, the society was never able to determine whether the information really came from the dead or whether the medium was extraordinarily gifted at telepathy. She herself remained uncertain regarding the source of her information. Interestingly enough, although she was amazingly accurate regarding events in the past and present, she never attempted to predict the future.

There are some documented examples of accurate predictions published before the events they described. Famous psychics such as Jeanne Dixon, Edgar Cayce, and Sylvia Browne have successfully predicted world events. However, they have also made predictions of events that never occurred. Why, then, do people still depend on them? What mathematician John Paulos calls the "Jeanne Dixon effect" is the tendency of believers to proclaim the correct predictions and ignore the misses. Tanya Luhrmann addresses the same problem in *Persuasions of the Witch's Craft*, citing Leon Festinger's work on cognitive dissonance to the effect that when theory and reality conflict, people will find ways to explain away the difference. When the ritual works, it proves that magic exists. When it does not, it must be because the energies were wrong or the ritual incorrectly performed.

What does this imply for the credibility of oracles?

Stories about oracles were preserved in ancient times because they proved a point or added to the dramatic impact of a story. Fictional oracles are always correct. In plays like *Oedipus Rex*, the efforts of King Laius to evade the prophecy that his son will kill him set in motion the events that lead to his death, and the efforts of Oedipus to discover the murderer whom the oracle has said is causing the city's misfortunes create the tragedy. The ambiguous prophecies of the three witches in *Macbeth* deceive the warrior into treason and then are fulfilled one by one to destroy him. In the Icelandic sagas, spae sessions introduce information or move the plot along. Even in the famous story of the Greenland völva, the ostensible reason for the spae session, which is to find out when the famine will end, is only a preliminary to the völva's prophecies regarding the future of one of the main characters, the girl who sings the invoking song.

The historical answers provided by the Delphic oracle are much more mundane. The majority consist of instructions or information rather than prophecies. And as we have seen above, the clearest prediction in this group—the first reply to the Athenians' question about the Persian invasion—was wrong. Apparently, however, Apollo sometimes gave a second opinion. The Athenians replied, "Give us a better oracle for our country; respect these suppliant boughs which we carry. Otherwise we shall not leave the adyton, but will stay here until we die."

"Pallas cannot appease Zeus with her many prayers," came the second answer. "But I shall tell you this immovable decree: all Attica will be taken, but Zeus grants Athena a wooden wall that shall alone be untaken and will help you and your children. Do not await the onset of cavalry and infantry from the continent at your ease, but turn about and leave. You will face them sometime again. O divine Salamis, you will lose many children of men either at sowing time or at harvest" (Quasi-historical answer 147). This answer, though ambiguous, was taken as symbolic and interpreted to mean not the wooden wall the Athenians built between the city and the harbor, but the wooden sides of the ships with which they defeated the Persian fleet at the Battle of Salamis.

If the oracle at Delphi did not see *the* future, what did she see? Given the vast difference between the resources of Persia and Greece at the time, the destruction of Athens was certainly the most likely outcome of the invasion. It is my belief that what the oracle saw was *a* future, the one most probable at the time. And perhaps the stubborn determination that sent the Athenians back to ask again changed the odds or enabled the seeress to surmount her own fears and thus see another possibility.

The idea that what an oracle predicts is probabilities also provides an explanation for the ambiguous answer sent to King Croesus. The test question could be answered because it referred to an event that had already taken place. However, which empire failed when Lydia and Persia did battle would depend on mutable factors, such as the skill of the generals and the fighting spirit of the men—on *choices,* in other words, that had not yet been made.

My own experience with oracle work suggests that straightforward predictions of the future are, if not impossible, rare or unlikely. There have been times when a question elicited an overwhelming response of "No!" or "Yes!" But it is far more common to hear the answer cast in the conditional. In one session, a man said that he had received predictions of danger if he returned home from the festival via car. In answer, the seer thundered, "If you drive through the desert, you will die!" Fortunately, we did not find out if this was an accurate prediction, since the questioner was so impressed by this second opinion that he took a plane home instead.

We only know if answers were accurate when people come back and tell us, and not too surprisingly, they usually tell us only when they are pleased with the results. One question for which we did have follow-up, and that also illustrates the utility of getting a second opinion, is reported by Lorrie Wood:

> A woman came to one of our smaller seidh sessions, where perhaps half a dozen people might show up. Her father was in poor health, and she asked the seer what might be done about it. The seer replied that the querent should have a talk with her mother to ensure that everything was being properly taken care of.
>
> A few weeks later, I and another member of our team happened to be in a metaphysical bookstore in a town some fifty miles south

of our usual haunt, and came across the same woman there. She told me that she had called her parents and that, while her mother had told her not to worry and certainly not to drive five hundred miles, her parents weren't the sort of people who wanted her to worry about them—and so, she wanted a rune reading as a second opinion.

Among the runes I drew were kenaz (fire) and mannaz (human-kind). Using the runes as a springboard, I dropped into an oracular trance and told her that her parents' caretakers were not doing their job, and she should call not her parents but the several medical professionals who were taking care of them straightaway and work out what was really going on. It seemed to me, further, that those same medical professionals were not necessarily motivated to do their job: I saw that the father was being overly stoic and the mother overly trusting, and I communicated all of this information to the querent. However, the key phrase that I repeated, over and over, based on the runes I had pulled, was "Light a *fire* under their *asses!*" This done, I returned to myself. She thanked me for my answer, and I didn't—at the time—think any more of it.

Nearly a year later, I was unpacking my car at Pantheacon, the local annual pagan convention. A woman I didn't immediately know ran up to me—"You! *You!* Hey! Wait a minute!"—obviously delighted to see me. I put down my bag and smiled cheerfully (if cluelessly).

"You! I have no idea how to thank you! *You saved my father's life!*"

Well, we're trained not to remember the answers we've given unless the querents happen to remind us what they were, so I was caught rather flat-footed. "Really? That's great! Er . . . how did I do that? Did I give you an answer at seidh or something?"

"You gave me a rune reading! Don't you remember?"

I found that I could—at that time, I could count all the rune readings I'd done on one hand—so I immediately remembered the bookstore. "Oh! Oh, yes! And what happened?"

"Well, I tried calling again but I couldn't get hold of anyone, and my mother kept telling me not to worry. So I got in my car and drove down there, and it was *exactly* as you said. His doctor wasn't paying attention to him [her father] at all, and my mother trusted him too much to look for a second opinion. So I got another doctor to have a look at him, and sure enough, he had something wrong that needed to be treated right away or it would have killed him! You saved my father's life!"

Of course, I'd hardly done any such thing—it was the daughter's own desire for a second *medical* opinion that did so—but that, in turn, had come from that same skeptical daughter's desire for a second *divinatory* opinion. On reflection, I think this speaks better to the strength of her character than anything *we* did. At the time, I was so flat-footed I wouldn't even think of asking for something in return, but nowadays, I've found that it's best to let a querent pay you back *something* if they feel well served, even if it's just a drink at the hotel bar.

THE CASE FOR TELEPATHY

How did the famed oracles of old get their results, and how do seers and psychics get information today? In his book on the Delphic oracle, Professor Dempsey comes to a rather ambiguous conclusion:

> Perhaps it [prophecy] is to be explained by the laws of telepathy, for, especially under abnormal psychic conditions, persons have shown themselves endowed with a knowledge truly marvelous. These abnormal psychic conditions, in the case of the Pythia, would probably be induced to a certain extent by the course of mantic preparation which she had to perform. The fasting, the drinking from the sacred spring, the chewing of the laurel leaves—these, combined above all with a *strong belief in the reality of the inspiration,* might in a guileless, uneducated soul—especially a woman—produce such an abnormal psychic state, which could induce even the physical phenomena of trance and agitation, such as were associated with the Delphi priestess. (Dempsey 1918, 72)

Aside from the fact that the pythia did not, in fact, answer in a state of agitation, nor were all the prophets of the Classical world female, I believe that the "course of mantic preparation," training, and faith in the process can indeed make it possible for most of those who feel called to do the work of an oracle. Certainly almost every one of the seers I know has had at least one experience in which an answer included information that, without some kind of rapport with the questioner, he or she could not know. Winifred Hodge Rose comments on an answer she gave to a woman who wanted to start her own business and was debating which of two different things she should choose.

> She didn't say anything about either one. Very unusually, my first impression of the answer was a smell—a good smell, like flowers. I then saw people coming into a pleasant place, reading books, and feeling at home. For the second, I also got a good smell, this time like unusual but delicious food, and a sense of hospitality. It turned out she was debating between opening a metaphysical bookstore, which would sell incense and essences, and starting a catering business! Again, these are not things one could get simply by guesswork. . . . Even with the business choice, where no ancestor was directly involved, there was a "reality check" by exposing me to the smell and feel of the different choices, to make sure the querent knew I was on track.

> It seems clear to me that some form of telepathy was at work in these and many similar instances. I could not possibly have guessed or imagined such detailed, correct information, and as you know, the way we do spaeworking precludes us from slyly observing people's expressions, body language, etc., to tell whether we're on the right track. We're in a dimly lighted space with dark veils over our heads and our eyes closed; we don't ask the querents leading questions or any questions at all, usually. The querent usually gives us no more than a sentence or two, with little information, and then we're on our own.

In an article written for the Society for Psychic Research, Andrew Lang compared the conversational interaction between Mrs. Piper and her clients with that of a Zulu seeress who asks probing questions of the querent in order to refine data. His general conclusion was that although there were many cases in which the medium could have gotten information by other means, there were also some in which the data was known only to the client. In others, the information apparently came from people in other parts of the world.

As Winifred Hodge Rose points out, in our own practice, the seer cannot see the querent and thus cannot read body language. When a question is asked of the dead, the seer does ask for a name and date and may explore further to focus identity, but in most cases, when the question is not addressed to a particular being, the answer comes without any cues from the querent.

One of the things that may make it easier to connect with a questioner is group energy, which can enliven or depress the ritual, just as audience reaction can deaden a play or carry it along. Even those who do not ask questions help with the singing, and their interest supports both seers and questioners. Jordsvin reports feeling depleted when too many people leave the hall before the end of the ceremony. Winifred Hodge Rose observes, "I have many times noticed that I get really stellar answers when the querent is accompanied by a number of other people who take great interest and concern in the question, thus beefing up the energy that 'feeds' me as I search for and interpret the answer."

Scientific studies of telepathy have been inconclusive. Although experimental subjects sometimes succeed, neither they nor seers, ancient or modern, bat a thousand all the time. Whatever is going on when we come up with such information, oracle work is clearly an art, not a science, and subject to influences we do not understand. Skeptics have proposed that successful psychics consciously or unconsciously use techniques such as cold reading, in which the psychic derives information from observing the client, or warm reading, in which the psychic makes statements that could actually apply to many people, and it is the subject who provides the meaning. In an article published in the *Skeptical Inquirer* (May 2004), former psychic reader Karla McLaren reported that she had developed a technique of unconscious cold reading through cultural osmosis. By stating her observations as questions rather than facts, she caused the questioner to "lean into the reading" and provide more information.

But observation, conscious or unconscious, cannot account for all the answers we have heard. Perhaps we can gain some insight by looking at the ways different states of consciousness are processed. In 1996, brain researcher Jill Bolte Taylor had a stroke that shut down the left hemisphere of her brain. Suddenly the mental monologue was silent, along with her awareness of herself as a separate being. Instead, she felt energy and euphoria. In a talk available on the TED network, she describes the functions of the two hemispheres:

> Our right hemisphere is all about this present moment. It's all about "right here, right now." Our right hemisphere, it thinks in pictures, and it learns kinesthetically through the movement of our bodies. Information, in the form of energy, streams in simultaneously through all of our sensory systems, and then it explodes into this enormous collage of what this present moment looks like, what this present moment smells like and tastes like, what it feels like, and what it sounds like. I am an energy being connected to the energy all around me through the consciousness of my right hemisphere. We are energy beings connected to one another through the consciousness of our right hemispheres as one human family. And right here, right now, we are brothers and sisters on this planet, here to make the world a better place. And in this moment we are perfect, we are whole, and we are beautiful.
>
> My left hemisphere—our left hemisphere—is a very different place. Our left hemisphere thinks linearly and methodically. Our left hemisphere is all about the past, and it's all about the future. Our left hemisphere is designed to take that enormous collage of the present moment and start picking out details, details, and more details about those details. It then categorizes and organizes all that information, associates it with everything in the past we've ever learned, and projects into the future all of our possibilities. And our left hemisphere thinks in language. It's that ongoing brain chatter that connects me and my internal world to my external world. (*www.ted.com/talks/jill_bolte_taylor_s_powerful_stroke_of_insight.html#*)

Mystics in many religions have described having feelings while in meditation that are similar to Taylor's description of right-brain experience. Perhaps the techniques that we use to achieve a receptive state in oracle work activate the right hemisphere of the brain to a level at which it can access that unifying energy. At the same time, we maintain sufficient access to our left-brain capacities to process what we receive from that connection and communicate what we perceive.

As one of our seers once answered a gentleman who asked about the cause of crop circles, "Some are the result of natural phenomena or human action—and some are not." Without further research and experimentation, we cannot be certain how seers get information about things they could not possibly know. However, I agree with Dr. Taylor that there is an energy that connects us, and it may be this energy that seers sometimes access when in oracular trance.

RECEPTIVITY AND RESPONSIBILITY

To gain full benefit from an oracular experience, not only the seer, but also the questioners should be in a state of receptivity in which disbelief is suspended. We may not require perfect love, but the seer has to trust that there will be an answer, that what she perceives is coming from somewhere beyond her own subconscious, and that it will be useful to the questioner even if she herself never finds out what it means. The questioner has to trust that the seer is telling the truth as she sees it and listen with his heart as well as his ears. There is no one so deaf as the man who refuses to hear. For the duration of the session, both parties need to suspend their disbelief. Trying to second-guess or analyze the process in the middle will tangle the threads. When all is working well, one insight leads on to another until the inspiration peaks, and ideas and information weave themselves into a new tapestry of meaning.

But then comes a second stage, in which intuition must make way for interpretation. In oracle work, we are required only to postpone judgment, not to throw it out entirely. In *Viga-Glum's Saga*, Glum processes a significant dream by turning it into poetry and then discussing it with a friend. Once we have experienced the moment of insight fully, we shift from right- to left-brain thinking and examine it.

When you have received an oracular answer, consider sharing it with a trusted friend and exploring what it might mean. If your answer recommends action or a decision, *get a second opinion from a qualified professional!* If the question is personal or spiritual, consulting another diviner can throw some light on the meaning. If the answer was about your health, check any advice with a doctor or nutritionist. If it was about legal action, consult a lawyer.

Be especially careful if the seer or psychic you have consulted requires you to pay more money to deal with dangers the first session has revealed. A fair recompense for the expenditure of time and energy is reasonable. Ever-increasing requests for payments suggest fraud.

THE ORACLE AS COUNSELOR

When we look at the questions people actually have asked, both in the past and present, it is clear that most of the time what they want to know is not what will happen so much as what *is* happening and what they should do about it.

Charles Babbage, inventor of the first "computer," once observed, "On two occasions I have been asked, 'Pray, Mr. Babbage, if you put into the machine wrong figures, will the right answers come out?' . . . I am not able rightly to apprehend the confusion of ideas that could provoke such a question" (Babbage 1864, 67). A more modern version of this is the concept known as GIGO—"garbage in, garbage out." The same principle might be applied to the work of an oracle.

Although at times a saturation of probabilities may precipitate prophecy in the awareness of a talented seer, in general, the oracle cannot answer until there is a question. Furthermore, the accuracy of the answer may depend on the care with which the query was framed, as its depth is determined by the degree of need. A frivolous question elicits no answer, a frivolous answer, or more usually, a snarky set-down from the seer.

Sometimes, the effectiveness of an answer depends less on its content than on the receptivity of the questioner. The skeptics who seek to deconstruct telepathy assume that "leaning into the reading" devalues it. I would propose the opposite—that unless the questioner participates and contributes to the process, a reading or answer cannot truly reach him. The elaborate setups at Delphi and Claros were intended to affect the questioners as well as the seers. In a mundane setting, the best advice, whether it comes from your mother or an oracle, may go in one ear and out the other. Just as scenery, lighting, and music help the audience to suspend its disbelief at a play, the theatrical elements in an oracular setting and ritual predispose the questioners to pay attention.

By the time they had climbed halfway up Mount Parnassus to Delphi, or crawled through the blue marble tunnel at Claros, pilgrims were ready for marvels. In Scandinavia, the special preparations for the reception of the völva predisposed people to pay attention. When a participant leaving the hall comments that it was "just like something out of *National Geographic*," we know we have created a setting in which people can believe that we know what we're doing. It seems to me that impromptu seers have a harder job. Queen Maeve might not have listened no matter how the prophecy was given, but though the *ban-drui* Fedelm was able to *see*, the queen, reining in her horses on the road to ruin, did not *hear*.

In this book, the focus has been on the work of the seer, but in a ritual context, prayers and song, group expectation, and the safety of a warded setting combine to create a receptive state of mind in the questioners. When, as often happens, the answer comes as a vision and is cast in imagery, even the seer may have no idea what it means. At one event, the questioner said only that she had several options and wanted to know which one she should choose. The answer was, "Orange." Afterward, she explained that she had color-coded her options, but she never did tell us what they were.

Through the pythia, Apollo instructed questioners on what sacrifices to make and what gods to honor, how to deal with family matters, where to find healing, and where to found new colonies and look for alliances. Today, seers advise people on work, health, housing, and relationships with humans and gods. Many of the answers I hear given from the chair are, in essence, the same good advice a counselor would give—sometimes, the advice the questioner herself would come up with if someone else asked her the same question. It is the ritual setting and energy that make the difference. Because the questioner receives the response from the seer, she "leans into" the question, opens her ears to truly *hear* the answer, and makes it her own.

An oracular ritual helps participants to open up to wisdom, but if we are willing to look for it, life is suffused with meaning. Not everyone is called to see for other people, but all of us have the capacity to connect with the flow of energy in the world around us and obtain wisdom for ourselves.

Part Two

INVOKING THE ORACLE

I

PREPARATION

THE SKILLS OF A SEER

To do oracular work, what skills do you really need?

Just as gifted musicians spend hours training muscles and honing technique even born seers can do the work better when they understand what they are doing and why. The exercises that follow will help you to develop the skills that experienced seers identify as important. They include getting into and out of trance, connecting with the questioner, getting and communicating information while remaining in trance, and perceiving spirits and dealing with them safely. Sample journeys offer practice in moving around in inner space. The discussion of ritual roles and responsibilities will help you to organize oracle sessions, and the rituals will serve as models.

Oracle work is an advanced practice. With support and protection from a trained team, a receptive but inexperienced seer can provide good answers. In our workshops, we can give most participants a taste of what it's like to do so, but we've found that the people who can work as independent oracles immediately are those who already have training in related practices, such as meditation or shamanic counseling. If you are new to these disciplines, you will need to master them before tackling the exercises here. If you are experienced, consider taking the time to do a review. If an individual or, better still, a group, first works through the skills covered in *Trance-Portation*, they can then use the material in *The Way of the Oracle* to refine and add the skills they will need to serve as oracles in their communities. But even if you are not interested in seeing for others, these exercises can help you to develop your intuition and ability to find meaning in the world.

The following exercises are presented roughly in the order in which these skills would be needed in an oracular session; however, except for the first two, you can work on them in whatever order is convenient for you.

KNOW THYSELF

"Know thyself" was one of the precepts posted at Delphi. "Accept your strengths and weaknesses." "Trust." "Get out of your own way." Stated in various ways, this advice came from all the seers I questioned.

The first step in oracular training is to honestly identify your own strengths and needs. If you have worked with *Trance-Portation*, you have already filled out a questionnaire something like this one. You need to know you have the basic skills before you can move on. But not all the questions are the same, and in any case, you will now be answering from a different perspective. There are no right or wrong answers. Your responses will help you figure out what kinds of training you need.

Exercise 1.1. Self-Evaluation Before Beginning Oracle Training

1. What is your experience with trance states?

✦ What traditions of trance or meditation have you practiced? How long?

✦ Which one(s) did you find most compatible, and which seemed unsympathetic?

✦ In each case, do you understand why?

Analyzing your experience with trance will tell you what skills you bring to the work.

2. What do you know about the following?

✦ Relaxation and breath control. (These skills help the seer to open up to information. For exercises that will help you develop them, see Chapters 1 through 3 of *Trance-Portation*.)

+ Visualization. (For exercises that will help you to perceive, focus, remember, and articulate what you need to develop them, see Chapters 1 through 3 of *Trance-Portation*.)

+ Lucid dreaming. (If you can direct your dreams, you can direct your journeys.)

+ Self-hypnosis. (You can adapt this process to put yourself into oracular trance.)

+ Solo journeying. (This is one way to seek information while in trance. For exercises, see Chapters 5 and 8 of *Trance-Portation*.)

+ Leading path workings. (This is especially useful when guiding others. For ways to do it better, see Appendix II of *Trance-Portation*.)

+ Shamanic healing. (This practice provides useful experience in working with spirits.)

+ Divination—what kind? (Experience in interpreting symbols in one kind of divination can transfer to another.)

+ Interpreting omens (experience in opening up to information).

+ Drawing down, aspecting, or deity possession (experience in channeling information from a spiritual source).

+ Folk magic. (Sometimes the answer involves giving the querent instructions or a spell.)

+ Mythology. (List the pantheons and cultures you know well enough to identify deities and symbols. You should only attempt to contact/answer questions about deities about whom you have some knowledge. A good resource is Joseph Campbell's *Masks of God*.)

+ Shamanism. (Experience with shamanic practices can often be converted to oracular practice, though they are not the same.)

✦ Jungian psychology. (Jung's perspective on the meaning and nature of dreams and other symbolism can help you to interpret the things you see in vision.)

All of these will give you a context within which to understand the work of the seer and help you to interpret the images you may encounter.

3. **Have you ever had a voluntary or involuntary psychic experience?**

✦ More than once?

✦ Did you perceive information about someone else that you could not have known through ordinary means? Was that information confirmed?

✦ Did you receive information or images about a future event, and do you know if that event came to pass?

✦ What were the circumstances in which this event occurred?

✦ How did you react? If others were aware of it, how did they react to you?

✦ How do you feel about the possibility of such experiences occurring again?

Some people are drawn to oracle work because they have had such experiences, and others because they would like to. If you are the former, analyzing what happened will help you predict how you are likely to react to formal training.

4. **Do you have a power animal, totem, or spirit guide? How did you acquire it? How often do you contact it, or how does it contact you?**
Although working with an inner guide, especially in animal form, is more characteristic of shamanism than oracular practice, having a helper on the "inside" can be extremely useful. For help in finding

and working with such a guide, see Chapters 6 and 7 of *Trance-Portation*.

5. Do you have a strong affinity with/devotion to specific gods and/or goddesses? How did you meet them? How often do you contact them, or how do they contact you?

The Greek oracles and prophets in many other lands were the "voices" of the gods. Those who have strong relationships with deities are more likely to channel them. Understanding how such relationships work will make it easier to answer "god questions."

6. What is your general state of health? Do you have any chronic or cyclical problems or conditions (especially heart or blood-pressure issues, diabetes, menstrual or menopausal symptoms, etc.) that affect your mood, energy, or focus? Are you on any medications?

The care that was taken to protect and prepare the pythia and other oracles before and after a session is evidence that this work can be stressful. The seer must be realistic about his or her physical condition and refuse to work if he or she is not in good health.

7. Have you been in counseling? What kind and for what? What areas and topics are likely to produce an emotional reaction in you?

In oracular trance, one is vulnerable to the emotions of the questioner. If a question hits an issue about which you have strong feelings, you may be hurt and will be unlikely to give a detached answer. If you know where your "buttons" are, you can refuse to answer certain questions. For more work in this area, see Exercise 1.2.

8. How do you react to alcohol or drugs? Have you ever taken any psychoactive drug or hallucinogen? How did it affect you?

Although drugs are not necessary to reach an altered state, they can propel you into one. Drug experience may give you an idea how you might react to trance.

9. Have you ever had a life-threatening accident or illness? Did you have any unusual experiences during the crisis? Did it change your attitude toward life?

Such experiences are common in shamanic traditions. They may also point you toward spiritual work of other kinds.

10. Do you belong to a circle, kindred or coven, or other spiritual group? Does it practice trance work or meditation? If so, what kinds? How often? For what purposes?

Oracle work, unlike mysticism, is usually a group activity. You will learn and practice the skills more easily if you train with a team.

11. Are any other group members working with this book? Will your group support your efforts to master these skills? Is this group part of a wider community that an oracle group might serve?

In order to give answers, you need people who will ask questions and be a support team.

12. What are your goals in beginning this training? Why do you want to learn how to do oracle work? In what context do you see yourself using this skill?

This is the critical question. Try to visualize yourself acting as an oracle. Whom are you serving? What will you get out of it? What will they?

Exercise 1.2. Releasing Traumas

People seek oracles because they have decisions to make, problems to solve, relationships to heal, and issues to resolve. They come seeking guidance and an opinion from a neutral source. If the answers were easy, they would not need an oracle, but an issue that is traumatic for a questioner may also get a strong response from the seer.

You have to be honest with yourself as well as with the questioner. To avoid being taken by surprise when a querent's problem or emotion presses one of your buttons, you need to know what and where they are. A medical student has to deal with his own feelings about physical pain before he can treat patients. In the same way, even if seers have not dealt with all their own issues, they should recognize what kinds of questions will affect how they respond.

Here are some life issues and crises that can provoke strong reactions. Consider them and answer the questions. Take your time—one category per week may be enough. If you uncover more trauma than you expected, seek counseling. It is a sign of courage, not weakness, to recognize hang-ups and take steps to deal with them.

Relationships

Describe your best and worst memories of each of the people listed below. What resentments do you need to release? What wrongs need to be made right? Do you need to apologize? Acknowledge a mistake? Offer compensation? Or do you need that from others?

Mother, father, sister, brother, children, lover(s), husband or wife, coworkers or boss

Life Crises

What experience (if any) have you had with each of the following? How did it affect you? How did you deal with it? How does thinking about it make you feel?

Death of a loved one, desertion by a loved one, abortion/miscarriage, unemployment, bankruptcy, losing a home, physical or mental abuse, rape, physical violence, post-traumatic stress disorder

Health

People often ask about health issues. Some of the scariest are listed below. Describe what your experience (if any) has been with each, whether it affected you or someone close to you. What was the outcome? How does thinking about it make you feel?

Cancer, diabetes, heart trouble, weight, Alzheimer's, stroke, mental retardation, mental disease, HIV/AIDS

Emotions

What things make you happy? Describe an experience that filled you with joy. What makes you sad? Describe your greatest grief; how did you feel? What makes you angry? Describe a time when you were so mad you committed physical violence—or wanted to.

How often do you experience extreme emotions? Do you know what physical or psychological factors affect your reactions? When you feel strongly, how do you deal with your feelings?

BECOMING THE ORACLE

As we have seen, many oracular traditions include a formal or informal process of purification and transformation in which the seer withdraws from ordinary life before the oracular session or takes the time to align him- or herself with the local energies. Our lives today rarely offer the opportunity for such a complete preparation, but we can begin the process by showering and putting on clean clothing. If you are working within a culturally based tradition, such as the Hellenic or Heathen, wearing appropriate clothing will help you to make the transition from now to a time when oracles were an accepted part of the community. Whether or not you have specific garb, wear loose, comfortable clothing. A necklace or other jewelry that is only worn for oracular work will signal the unconscious that it is time to shift gears. Those who work with spiritual allies may wear some piece of jewelry that evokes their presence. If you are under the protection of a particular deity, wear a symbol of your faith. Some seers also find it useful to adopt a ritual name that they use only in this work. Hearing yourself addressed by this name is an additional cue to move into oracular trance.

Exercise 2.1. The Oracular Persona

This exercise can be done with a partner who directs you to take in each step and reads the path working to move you into trance, or you may tape or memorize the procedure and work alone. Experiment with cues, such as dabbing a particular essential oil under your nose or pulling a veil over your head.

✦ Ground, center, regularize your breathing, and move into the neutral trance state. (For this, see Chapters 1 through 3 of *Trance-Portation*.)

✦ Using the path working from the Core Oracle Rite in Part II, Chapter IV, or one that you have developed for your own practice, journey to the cavern or other setting where you find the archetypal oracle. (For journeying skills, see Chapters 5 and 8 of *Trance-Portation*.)

✦ Move forward until you can see the Seat of Seeing and visualize yourself sitting there, wearing your ritual clothes. How does this image differ from the one you see in the mirror? How is it the same?

✦ Ask the figure in the chair for its name.

✦ Move forward once more and merge your awareness with that of the figure on the chair. Feel yourself sitting there. Look around and note how the setting appears from this perspective.

✦ If you are working with a partner, when he has given you the previous instructions, he should ask you a question.

✦ When you have answered or when you feel it is time, rise from the chair and move to the entrance of the oracular site. As you pass through, let the persona of the seer fade away.

✦ Complete the journey back to ordinary reality, ground and center, open your eyes, and return to ordinary consciousness. Affirm your mundane name. Do a "checksum" (see Exercise 2.2 below) to make sure you are back to normal.

Exercise 2.2. Checksums

In computer engineering, checksums are information computed from digital data and used to compare results and identify accidental errors or corruptions that might have crept in during transmission or storage of the data. We use the term for an internal checklist that you can use to make sure that when you leave the seat of the seer, you're the same person as the one on your driver's license. Reverse the procedure you used to go into trance, breathing more quickly, moving fingers and toes, lowering psychic shields, withdrawing awareness within the boundaries of your body once more. As you develop your skills as an oracle, pay attention to your health and feelings. Not feeling like your "usual self" after trance work may indicate a problem. If you start to experience disturbed sleep, fatigue, emotional instability or illness, you may need to step back or slow down.

Exercise 2.3. Making the Offering

Oracular rituals often include offerings. In the *Havamál* 42, we are told that "a gift demands a gift again." Spiritual work is strengthened by an exchange of energy. A client who pays a psychic (within reason) is balancing the energy the psychic expends. Participants who sing for the seer at oracular seidh sessions raise energy that the seer will use to find answers. We offer our praise to the Powers who guide and guard us, and we offer money to pay for the use of the hall. We purify ourselves and our space before the ritual, and the members of the ritual team link their energies.

But there is another, equally important gift: that of the seer who offers him- or herself to be a vehicle for the transmission of wisdom. Whether the dedication is a formal prayer or a simple "Please God, don't let me screw the pooch!" there needs to be a moment before the ceremony when you affirm your willingness to set aside your own will and do the work. Practice the prayer that follows, or write something that will fulfill the same purpose, until you have internalized the essence.

> *The Seat of Seeing I ascend*
> *To answer those who come in need.*
> *Powers of Truth, I am your voice*
> *To speak the words that they will heed.*
> *My human passions put aside,*
> *Surrender my identity,*
> *Until the holy work is done,*
> *and all may be restored to me.*
> *Clarity of sight I ask,*
> *Clarity of speech and spell,*
> *Understanding ears to hear,*
> *Protecting powers to ward us well.*
> *Oh, Powers of Truth, I am your voice*
> *Bring blessings from the words I say,*
> *Ward me as I fare within,*
> *Accept my offering today.*

CLEARING THE CHANNELS

By affirming your willingness to serve, you have laid the groundwork for clearing your mind. Essentially this involves shifting most of your consciousness from the left to the right hemisphere of your brain. The concept is simple—just let go of distractions and relax into a state of receptivity in which you have no personal thoughts, needs, or will—but this may be the hardest skill to learn. It is, however, a very useful state, a preparation not only for giving answers, but also for doing many kinds of psychic work, as well as for easing stress and renewing energy.

Pay special attention to silently counting your breathing. The advantage of this method is that you can use it anytime and anywhere, including in the middle of the oracular ritual when the preliminaries are past and it is time to switch gears and go to work. You will find more ways to approach this skill in Exercises 9 and 10 from *Trance-Portation*.

Exercise 3.1. Slow Breath, No Mind

✦ Find a place to work where you will not be distracted or disturbed. If you are working alone, secure the door and ward the space, or ask your partner to watch over you. You may want to set a timer or put on a piece of music that will last as long as you need.

✦ Stretch to release muscular tension, and take a position you can hold for an extended period, in a comfortable chair. Decide how long you want to spend on the exercise and set your mental alarm clock to tell you when it is time to return, or ask your partner to do so.

✦ Close your eyes, and affirm your intention to release all thoughts and concerns.

✦ Breathe in to a count of four, timing one beat per second (you can use a ticking clock to learn the pace). Hold for four beats, release your breath for four beats, and hold for four. Do not worry if you are still inhaling or exhaling during the second set of four beats. Do this until you have established a regular rhythm, mentally verbalizing the numbers. When extraneous thoughts intrude, recognize and dismiss them and return to counting. If counting is difficult, simply slow down each time you exhale.

✦ Now slow your breathing further. Take two seconds for each beat: "One . . . and . . . two . . . and . . . three . . . and . . . four . . . and . . ." Or try breathing slowly in and out to a count of twelve. Experiment, gradually pushing your limits. If you find yourself out of oxygen, take a deep breath and start again. Let the periods during which you are neither inhaling nor exhaling grow longer. Become still. Note at what point in this sequence you feel a change in awareness. This may manifest as a sinking feeling or a shift in orientation.

✦ When it is time to return, gradually make your breaths more quick and shallow, and as you near your normal pattern, stop counting and breathe less regularly. Yawn, sigh, open your eyes, and stretch. Consciously ground yourself once more.

Reading the induction below onto a tape will give you practice in clearing your mind. Gradually slow the pace.

> Sit in balance upon the earth.
>
> Let each limb relax.
>
> Here you are safe and secure.
>
> If there is need, you will be able to easily awaken and return.
>
> You hear sounds, but they mean nothing.
>
> All that does not concern you fades away.
>
> Anything you hear will only make it easier to look within.
>
> Let your eyes close.
>
> Breathe in . . . hold. . . .
>
> and out . . . hold. . . .
>
> Breathe in . . . hold. . . .
>
> and out . . . hold. . . .

Allow a minute or two to pass as you count your breaths.

> Now let the image of the place around you come to mind.
>
> Note the texture of the floor, then let that memory slip away.
>
> See the colors of the walls, and as you do so, watch them fade.
>
> Remember the placement of the furniture, then let shadow erase it all.
>
> Feel the temperature of the air, then withdraw awareness so that you feel nothing at all.
>
> All images and sensations begin to ripple and flow.
>
> All that you see, or hear, or feel dissolves and flows away.
>
> A thought comes to you.
>
> Recognize it, then let it go.

Again and again, all is carried away.

It all goes.

You are open and empty.

You need nothing.

You want nothing.

You have only to *be*.

Allow two to five minutes of silence, then gradually speak faster.

Reality is flowing around you.

You see light flickering on water.

You hear the ripple of a stream.

Gradually it gives way to an image of the room around you.

Feel your weight in the chair.

Twitch your fingers and toes.

Breathe in . . . and out . . . in . . . and out . . .

Let the air of that place become the air of this place.

Sigh and stretch, open your eyes,

and return.

Exercise 3.2. Answers in the Void

✦ Prepare and ward your space as before, then articulate a topic or problem to contemplate and set your inner alarm clock. Affirm that you will learn and remember what you need to know. If you are working with a partner, ask him or her to prepare a question.

✦ If you are training with cues, such as pulling down a veil or identifying yourself by your seer name, do so.

- Repeat the steps from Exercise 3.1 until you have reached the point at which you feel the shift.

- Take a few moments to settle into the receptive state, then allow the topic or problem to surface. If you are working with a partner, he or she should wait until your breathing has been regular for a while, then ask the question.

- Contemplate the topic or question. Sift the thoughts that come, and release those that don't seem relevant. Note what images persist and what associations emerge.

- When you have something concrete, fix it in your mind and alter your breathing to return.

- Ground yourself, and then report or write down results and insights.

- When you are comfortable reaching the open state by your favorite method, experiment with alternative approaches—counting breathing or not counting, working with or without cues, working with different cues, working outdoors, or working in a group.

TRANSITIONS

Another way to reach the oracular state is through internal sensory cues. For most people, visual imagery works well, but invoking the other senses can be equally powerful in energizing the right-brain. This method is especially useful when a ritual has already moved you into a somewhat altered state, and you need to make the transition to a deeper state in which you will be able to answer questions.

The unconscious mind speaks in symbols. By intentionally invoking and manipulating them, we can move our minds where we need them to be. Fantasy films and fiction are especially rich in such images. To stimulate your imagination, reread fairy tales or classics, such as the Narnia books of C. S. Lewis or Diane Duane's Young Wizard series, or watch films like *Matrix* or *Pan's Labyrinth*. You will find more on these skills in Chapter 4 of *Trance-Portation*.

Exercise 4.1. Passages

✦ Identify at least four kinds of ways to get from one area to another, such as a tunnel or passageway, a gate or door, a curtain or veil, a well or body of water through which one sinks, or a web, a forest, or other environment with multiple pathways. Feel free to add passages not listed here. If you are working in a tradition that already has a favorite passage image, add it to your list. For ideas, look at art books or travel or architectural magazines.

✦ Sensorize. Verbally or in writing, describe what it is like to pass through each one, using as many senses as you can. If you are artistic, add an illustration. If you are describing going through a veil or curtain, note not only the color and fabric, but the tactile sensation as it brushes your skin. Does it have a scent? Does the moving fabric make a sound?

✦ Choose one passage, close your eyes, and experience internally all the sensations of moving through it.

✦ Repeat the process with each of the other passages, and revise your descriptions to reflect what you have learned.

Exercise 4.2. The Oracular Doorway

✦ Choose a passage image, either one of your own that seems appropriate for oracular work or the one that your group uses.

✦ Ask a partner to lead you through the exercise. He or she should read the first four instructions from Exercise 3.1.

◆ When your breathing pattern has steadied, your partner should say:

> *NAME, NAME (your own or the oracle name you have chosen),*
> *the (name of passage, such as "the Gate") lies before you.*
> *Move forward now and pass through . . .*

◆ Your partner reads the description you have written, and you experience the sensations of going through.

◆ Your partner waits one to three minutes, then says:

> *NAME, it is time now for you to return.*
> *The (name of passage) lies before you,*
> *Come back to where I am waiting.*

◆ Experience the sensations of returning through the passage.

◆ Quicken your breathing and return to ordinary consciousness, and ground.

◆ When you have done this exercise with a partner often enough to internalize the process, practice it alone.

◆ When you are comfortable with the process, add questions.

BUILDING RAPPORT

A major difference between oracle work and most other trance work is that oracle work requires us to simultaneously connect to the Powers of the Otherworld and to human beings in this one. If oracles do, in fact, get many of their answers through telepathy, the ability to establish rapport with another mind is an essential skill. Parapsychology researchers experiment in a sterile laboratory environment in which subjects focus on neutral images. Our own experience has been that the most powerful results come when a question is fueled by need, an effect that is amplified when there is support from a community. The results of the exercises below may be experimentally biased, but possibly closer to the conditions of oracular practice.

These exercises should be repeated with several different partners. For more discussion on establishing rapport, see Chapter 9 of *Trance-Portation*.

Exercise 5.1. Sharing Images

✦ The transmitting partner selects an image to which he or she reacts strongly, such as a photograph of a loved one, a scene showing a place where he or she was happy or where he or she would love to go, or a picture that elicits other strong feelings.

✦ The partners sit back to back in a comfortable position, close enough so that they can sense each other's breathing. When they are settled, they close their eyes and match their breathing patterns. The transmitting partner counts out the rhythm until they synchronize.

✦ Once matched breathing is established, the partner with the image opens his or her eyes and contemplates the picture, paying particular attention to details while letting the emotion it evokes build.

✦ After a few moments, he or she closes his or her eyes again and starts to count breaths aloud once more, gradually increasing the pace to a normal waking rate. Both partners open their eyes and ground.

✦ The receiving partner writes down what he or she "saw" or perceived, shares impressions with the one transmitting, then looks at the image and refines the interpretation.

✦ Repeat with several other images in a row, moving from one to another while still in rapport and resynchronizing breathing between each one.

✦ Repeat in a group context while others raise energy by drumming, toning, etc.

✦ Repeat as a long-distance experiment, in which partners separated geographically sit to transmit and receive at an agreed upon time.

Exercise 5.2. Word Ball and Rap Battles

In the Old Norse *Havamál*, Odin says, "Word to word led me, Work to work led me" (141). Word Ball is a free-association game based on the same idea. Partner A starts with a word and partner B responds with the first word it suggests to her. Partner A responds with a word inspired by B's and so forth. It can also be played by a group going around a circle. Practice until everyone relaxes and the words flow freely. Notice if the words start to tell a story. To raise the energy and establish a rhythm, keep up a steady beat on a drum.

It was only after I had written this exercise that I realized that a "rap battle" is essentially the same thing. The poetry competition has an ancient lineage. Old Norse poets slung staves at each other, Druid bards could raise welts with invective, and medieval troubadours challenged each other to compete in complex poetic forms. In the rap battle, the background beat and the energy of the audience carry the combatants along as they use word association, rhyme, and rhythm to score verbal "hits."

Exercise 5.3. Advanced Interactive Journeying

If you have not done this before, begin with the form described in Exercise 5 in Chapter 9 of *Trance-Portation*, in which partners lie or sit near each other and narrate a joint path working, passing direction back and forth as they explore. Practice this with different partners until you often find yourself "seeing" images before your partners describe them.

When you are getting good results with this, journey with a partner to the oracle cave (see the journey script on page 176) or another oracular site of your choice, taking turns to describe the journey as before. When you arrive, one partner should ask a question, and the other should answer. Next, the one who answered may ask a question of his or her own while the first seeks an answer.

GUIDES AND SOURCES

The next set of exercises also requires experience in path working or spirit journeying. For basic journeying skills, review Chapters 5 and 8 of *Trance-Portation*.

In oracular work, animal allies or spirit helpers are not required, but they can be useful. Whether you develop a permanent relationship with such a figure or not, you may be called upon to seek out such beings in order to answer questions. The following exercises consist of a series of journeys to meet with them and introduce yourself.

Exercise 6.1. Acquiring an Ally

If you have done shamanic work, you will already have a spirit helper in animal form, but this being may or may not be interested in helping you with oracular work. Journey to ask, and if necessary, make another journey to find a second helper for this purpose. If you do not have a spirit helper and would like one, you will find instructions for acquiring and getting along with them in Chapters 6 and 7 of *Trance-Portation*.

Exercise 6.2. Meeting the Powers

One difference between the oracles of the past and the present is that, between then and now, the spiritualist movement changed the way we look for information. In the old days, people who wanted to contact the dead sat out on a grave mound or went to a necromanteion or a specialist like the Witch of Endor. However, the spiritualist and channeling movements are based on the assumption that we, like Odysseus and Aeneas, can go to the ancestors for counsel, and that assumption is now part of the popular consciousness. Thus, contemporary oracles often get questions for the dead and need to be prepared to answer them, as well as questions for other kinds of spirits and gods.

Practice by making (separate) journeys to contact a god, an ancestor, and a nature spirit. If you are working in a specific cultural tradition, review the descriptions of its Otherworld and use them as a map to guide your search. Or you may use the basic construct of an Upper, Middle, and Lower World. Nature spirits, animals, and beings such as dwarves can usually be found in the Lower World. Ancestors are usually located there also; however, I have had good luck contacting ancestral spirits through a grave mound in the Middle World. High elves and gods can be found in the Upper World, or you can seek a temple in the Middle World and invoke them there. The instructions below outline a journey to meet a goddess or a god.

Relax, breathe, and prepare to journey in your usual manner. Articulate your purpose, which is to meet a god or goddess or angelic power who can help you with oracular skills or provide information you need. If you are looking for a particular deity, build up in your mind's eye the appropriate environment. (If you are not already familiar with the terrain and architecture of your deity's culture, prepare by doing some research.) Or you can visualize a passage portal, and see what you find on the other side.

As you move through the Otherworldly landscape, look for a likely site for a temple, grove, or shrine, and let the image build up in your mind. Within this site, find a source of light, such as an altar flame or a shaft of sunlight. Imagine this bright glow taking human form until you see the goddess or god.

Greet the Power respectfully and ask your questions. When you have "spoken," open your awareness to receive an answer. It may come as words, as images, or as straight information—a certainty about what you are to do. You will have a sense when the communication is complete. Say thank you and visualize the deity becoming radiant light once more and then disappearing. Leave the temple and retrace your steps back to your base camp and so back to mundane reality.

If you will be working with the deity in your oracular practice, find a prayer from that Power's tradition to include in your ritual or create your own invocation or song. For an example of how this can work, see the Delphic Oracle Rite on page 168.

INFORMATION CAPTURE

When we trance for ourselves, it may be enough to have escaped ordinary consciousness. Transcendent insights can emerge in their own good time. But when we trance for others, we must be able not only to perceive, but also to focus and communicate what we find. You will find additional exercises on visualization and articulation in Chapter 4 of *Trance-Portation*.

Exercise 7.1. Sharpening the Senses

Select a physical object to contemplate. It should be big enough to hold in your hand and varied enough to interest you. Relax, breathe, and clear your mind. Then look at your object. What is its color, shape, decoration, texture, smell? Take a mental photograph. Then close your eyes and try to "see" the object with inner vision. Open your eyes and look at your object again. What did you miss? Contemplate the object and then close your eyes and try again. Do this until you have memorized your first object, then practice again with a second. Try this exercise with a number of objects, both familiar and unfamiliar, until you can remember most of the details on your first or second try.

Exercise 7.2. Emotional Memory

Think back a few years and bring to mind an incident that made a vivid impression. If you have trouble finding something in your own life, take a scene from a book or film. It should be something that affects you strongly, but not traumatically. Contemplate the incident, paying specific attention to sensory details. What can you see? What is the temperature of the air? What sounds can you hear around you? If you are in the scene, what are you wearing? Notice weight and texture. When the scene has played to its conclusion, return to ordinary consciousness and write down everything you

---

can remember. If you are working with an episode from a book, reread the passage and note where your experience was the same or different, and in particular, what sensory impressions you remember that were not explicitly stated.

Sometimes, however, it is hard to make sense out of what we see. Practicing finding a pattern in random data is one way to gain skill in extracting meaning from the confusion of impressions we may encounter in trance.

Exercise 7.3. Pattern Recognition

✦ A figure-ground image is a picture in black and white that can be interpreted as a white image or a black one, depending on which color you interpret as the foreground. The most famous example is the "Rubin vase." Practice looking at such images and adjusting your focus back and forth. Look at the image below, or Google "figure-ground picture" to find the Rubin vase and others like it.

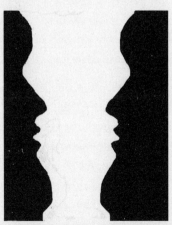

Figure and ground image

Another exercise based on optical phenomena involves the kinds of images found in the Rorschach test. You can make your own ink blots with poster paint and stiff paper, or work with photos of abstract art.

✦ Ground, center, move into the receptive state, and contemplate one of the images. What does it suggest?

✦ Have someone ask you a question, then repeat the process with a different image. Describe what it looks like, and then what it means.

✦ Distribute different images to the members of a group. After everyone grounds, relaxes, and moves into a receptive state, one person asks a question. The others contemplate their images, seek an answer, and write down what they get. When everyone has finished, return to ordinary consciousness and compare answers.

✦ Collect a handful of interesting stones. Practice casting them and interpreting the patterns they make.

Exercise 7.4. Interpreting Information

An interpreter of languages needs a good vocabulary in both tongues. An interpreter of oracles, whether the information comes from the ether or the questioner's mind, needs to be as knowledgeable as possible. Dion Fortune describes the problem in this way:

> [T]he communication brought through a medium depends to a large extent upon the capacity of the medium to act as a suitable channel. There are two aspects to this: one is the grade of the medium, which reflects the medium's own evolutionary development; and the other is the degree of education and general culture of a medium. If a medium is ill-educated and has few symbols available for the mind, then the inner-plane communicator can only work with what he has. (In Fielding and Collins 1985, 151)

I think that this is true whether one is channeling directly; relaying information from an ancestor, spirit, or deity; or recounting a vision. Even the most gifted seer cannot transmit effectively without the background to interpret and the vocabulary to describe what she sees. For example, a friend once went to a psychic who saw her surrounded by "men in bathrobes" who were throwing balls. This image confused the seer, but my friend, who had been in the military, easily identified them as Arabs throwing grenades.

The writings of Carl Gustav Jung and Joseph Campbell, as well as the book *The Golden Bough,* will give you a good general perspective on archetypal images. Seers who limit their work to specific religious communities, such as Christian, Heathen, or Hellenic, need to steep themselves in the theology and lore of their faith.

One way to practice interpreting information is by answering questions about archetypes while in trance. Ask a partner to look through a book on myth or archaeology until he finds an image that appeals to him. When you have achieved a receptive trance, your partner should describe the image and picture it in his mind and then ask you to explain what it means.

Exercise 7.5. Opening Up to Omens

When the exiled duke of Shakespeare's *As You Like It* speaks of finding "tongues in trees, books in the running brooks, sermons in stones," he is affirming (or perhaps trying to persuade himself) that roughing it in the wilderness is better than life at court because it enables him to perceive reality. To seek omens in everything is superstition. To find meaning in nothing is death. As with all spiritual work, we need to find a balance in which left- and right-brain thinking are put to their proper use. That said, opening up to omens is not only good training for seeing meaning, but also trains us to move easily in and out of the oracular state.

In the old days, one of the most common ways to divine was by the flight of birds. Today we have a variety of other options. In radiomancy, the answer is indicated by the first song to come up when you turn on the radio (this works best with a general popular or light-rock station, unless your life really is like a bad country music song). Bibliomancy gives you omens from words picked at random from a dictionary, Bible, or other weighty tome. A *cledon* is the old Greek name for chance-heard words that provide the answer to a question. Omens can also be found in commercials, on billboards, or in any of the myriad other communications that bombard us daily.

Before you seek an omen, center your energy, breathe, and move into a lightly altered state. When you have found the omen, note your conclusions, and then ground and return to ordinary consciousness. Here are some ways to practice.

✦ Ground, center, breathe, and articulate the question. Ask the universe or the Powers you honor to grant you an omen that will provide an answer.

✦ Each morning, pull a Tarot card or rune. Ask how it relates to your situation. During the day, be on the lookout for events, observations, conversations, etc., that will reflect the rune or card's meaning. Write down any insights at the end of the day.

✦ Ask a question. Pick up your book, turn on the radio, or go out and look and listen until something strikes you with the force of significance. The image or turn of phrase that you have noted is the stimulus for your unconscious to free associate until you have an answer.

✦ Ask a question and then go to a coffee shop or someplace where people are talking. Drink your coffee, focusing on its taste, and wait for some snatch of overheard conversation to strike you as significant.

✦ Ask a question and turn on the radio. Look for meaning in the title, lyrics, or associations of the song. This can work with commercials as well.

◆ Interpret the answer. In some of the sagas, a man who has a significant dream will write a stave of poetry to express it and then discuss its meaning with a friend. Talking or writing about your "omen" will help you to perceive it more clearly and lead you to an understanding of its meaning.

INFORMATION DELIVERY

The great Greek theatrical tradition grew out of Greek religion. The same thing happened again when religious plays performed outside the church or in the marketplace evolved into theater and eventually produced Shakespeare. Shamanic healing sessions feature dance, song, and costumes, and even the gypsy fortune-teller is likely to put up a few exotic decorations. Presentation is important. Even when you are working one-on-one, your manner and the way you deliver your information will affect the questioner's ability to receive it. Effective delivery is even more important when you are working in front of a crowd in a big public ritual. A memorable answer depends not only on what you say, but also how you say it.

Exercise 8.1. Bicameral Consciousness

Speaking oracles requires first that you are able to talk while in trance. For many, this may be the hardest part of the process. We are accustomed to think of trance work as a right-brain activity that takes place inside our heads. Language is handled by the left hemisphere, and being spoken to is likely to jerk us out of trance. But if we are to give answers, we must learn how to remain in trance while at the same time communicating with the outside world. We must teach the right and left hemispheres of the brain to share control. We know it is possible—hypnotists hold conversations with their subjects, and shamans report on their trance journeys while dancing around a fire and beating a drum.

One way this can be accomplished is to use the techniques of hypnotic induction to manage the trance, choosing one cue to draw the seer up to a level where he can communicate and another to send him back into deep trance. But even with this kind of support from the guide, the seer needs to be able to split consciousness. People do something like this when they carry on a conversation while simultaneously listening to music and driving a car. Leading a group discussion also requires one to split awareness in several directions.

Ease into it gradually by working with a partner. The interactive trance journey not only develops rapport, but it also gets you accustomed to reporting your inner experience. As you make the journey to an inner-world site, such as the Oracle Cave, your partner should periodically ask you what you are seeing. After you have received the cue to pass into a deeper, oracular trance, the connection that has been established will make it easier to respond when your partner asks a question. You can practice alone by recording your journeys on a tape recorder. Given practice, speaking in trance will not be a problem.

Exercise 8.2. Conditioned Responses

Once you *can* speak while in trance, you have to find the right words. In the old days, poets had the same challenge when they chanted epics in the halls of kings. The story was known, but much of the wording was improvised and changed each time they told the tale. They made their job easier by including stock phrases to bridge gaps and signal transitions. In the oracular poems of the Elder Edda, we find traces of what may be the same technique.

In *The Dream of Baldr*, Odin uses the same phrase, "Be not silent, Völva, thou will I question, until I know all that I want," to introduce each query, and the Völva replies, "Need made me speak, now must I be silent" to indicate the end of an answer. In other poems, she is apparently in a better mood and replies, "Much have I said, and can say more that you need to know. Will you hear further?" (*Shorter Seeress' Prophecy*) or "Would you know more, or what?" (*Völuspá*). Since these scenes are presented as poetry, which also relies strongly on repetition, we cannot be sure they are based on ritual; however, poetry is one of the most useful tools for creating ritual, being both incantatory and easy to remember, so there is no reason not to use these techniques in an oracle session. In Seidhjallr's practice, we adapt the lines as "Cease not seer, 'til said thou hast. Answer the asker 'til all he (or she) knows" to cue the seer to answer, and "This you know, would you know more?" to let the guide know the answer is finished.

I strongly recommend developing stock phrases that are appropriate to the style and cultural context in which you are working and incorporating them into your own oracular practice, both as cues to which you can condition yourself to respond and as poetic phrasing (see below).

Exercise 8.3. Prophecy and Poetry

Why did the oracle at Delphi (sometimes) speak in verse? Why did the Norse warrior Glum turn his dream into poetry? Perhaps it was because poetry uses language in a way that signifies more than the simple meaning of the words, and so do oracles. This is not to say that seers should always deliver their answers in neat hexameters, but one reason for presenting oracles in a ritual format is to put the questioners into a receptive frame of mind. Anything that makes an answer more impressive will make it more effective. Consider these examples:

1. (Delivered in an offhand tone.) "Your girlfriend's a bitch who's messing you up, you know. Maybe it's time to ditch her."

2. (Delivered in measured tones.) "The lady you love is a hound who tears at your heart. Though you love her, you must slip the leash and let her go."

They are the same advice, but if you are looking for spiritual counsel, which would impress you more?

Of course, most people can't speak poetically when fully conscious, so how are you supposed to do it in trance? If you can internalize poetic language and associate it with oracle work, hearing the cues will not only put you into trance, but it will also activate that style of speaking as part of your oracular persona.

✦ We learn language by hearing and imitating. Listen to recordings of good readers—people who love language and get the full value out of poetry that is rich in sound as well as sense. Get the *Oxford Book of English Verse* and practice reading aloud. Concentrate on poetry written before the mid twentieth century. Modern verse tends to be composed for the eye, not the ear.

✦ If you are working within a specific culture, read good translations of its poetry aloud and memorize selections. If you are Heathen, practice reading the three oracular poems in the Edda. (For this purpose, Hollander's translation provides the most poetic model, although he sometimes sacrifices fidelity to euphony.)

✦ Extemporize poetry. When you see or experience something noteworthy, take a moment to express your response to it in poetic language, even if it's not formal verse. Express the perceptions of all your senses, not just vision.

✦ Move into oracular trance. Have a partner ask you to describe a scene in the real world that you know well. Then say something significant about it. Travel to various locations in the Otherworld and describe what you find there.

Exercise 8.4. Long-Distance Diction

"Seeress, you speak to us from a far country, and your voice is faint. Will you give us your answer again?"

This cue was not originally part of our ritual, but sometimes it is necessary. You can give answers that would turn the pythia green with envy, but you might as well be talking to yourself if they cannot be heard. Even when you are working one-on-one, a mumbled answer can be hard to comprehend, and in a public ritual, projection and clarity are essential.

Surprisingly, the first seeress I needed to remind in this way was a professional singer who in ordinary life was an outgoing and always audible personality. Apparently knowing *how* to project is not enough. You also have to persuade your body to cooperate when you are in trance. Oracular communications must be articulated clearly and voiced with enough volume for everyone to hear.

To Develop Volume

Begin by sitting up straight and filling up with as much air as you can. Put one hand on your belly and the other opposite it, on your back. Take in enough air to make both hands move. Tighten the muscles just beneath your rib cage to exhale smoothly but strongly. Practice this until you can identify the sensation clearly. Combine deep breathing with counting.

Stand in a large space. Breathe in, and as you breathe out, say the first letter of the alphabet. Breathe in again, and this time, say "B," aiming your voice to hit a little farther away. Continue with the alphabet, aiming farther still with each letter. If you get lightheaded, stop and breathe normally for a time and then continue. But the time you reach "Z," you will have internalized the rhythm. Try this with a friend to make sure you are reaching the distance you are aiming at. Practice once a day until you can automatically pitch your voice to whatever distance you choose.

If your ritual does not include some singing, find another way to warm up your voice. Before the ritual begins, do a sound check by standing next to the oracle's seat and projecting your voice to the farthest row. Speak for long enough to get a sense of how much force you will need. Internalize how that feels and silently affirm that when you are sitting as seer you will pitch your voice to be heard.

To Develop Clarity

Begin by reading poetry into a tape recorder and playing it back. If you have not done this before, the way you sound may surprise you. Listen critically, noting if any vowels or consonants are unclear. Do you drop the ends of words or run them together? Does your volume remain consistent? Are there any other characteristics that might make you hard to understand?

The philosopher Demosthenes practiced public speaking with a mouthful of pebbles. You can do the same thing with a pencil held horizontally between your teeth. Practice repeating tongue twisters. For a selection, see *www.uebersetzung.at/twister/en.htm*.

After you have worked on your diction for a time, read the same passage of poetry you used for a test into the recorder and listen to the result. Note where you still need work, and continue practicing.

When preparing for a ritual, speak your prayer of dedication (see Exercise 2.3) as clearly as you can. Internalize that feeling and affirm that as the seer you will speak so that all can understand.

LETTING GO

It is not enough to get an answer. You also have to be able to let it go. The last line of *Völuspá* is "Now she sinks." When I am in oracular trance, I experience the sequence of questions as a regular lift and descent, in which the question stimulates vision and the end of the answer allows me to sink into the neutral, receptive state once more. But sometimes a vision does not want to let go. The following exercise can help you to detach.

Exercise 8.5. Detachment

Watch a film or read a story that you know will elicit a strong reaction. When you feel yourself growing emotional, hit pause or close the book. Hold the scene in your mind. Identify what you are feeling and try to figure out why it makes you feel that way. What factors in your life might explain your feeling? When you have explored your reaction, intentionally allow the image to fade and let the emotion go. Note how it feels to do this. After practicing, try it when you get stuck in traffic or have an argument with your significant other.

II

JOURNEYS

Journeys, in the form of guided meditations or path workings, are a common feature in neo-pagan rituals and neo-shamanic practice today. They were not, however, a standard element in the oracular rituals of the past, nor is journeying the only way to find answers. Even when a journey has been the means by which the seer reaches the oracular state, the information often comes directly or as a vision in response to the question.

That said, the inner journey has a number of uses. When a question concerns an Otherworld figure, we can journey to find and speak with him, her, or it. If an answer is slow in coming, we can journey in search of information. And, as indicated above, a journey can help us to move into trance or to connect to a specific cultural sector of the collective unconscious. Spirit journeying is, therefore, a useful skill, whose mechanics are covered in detail in Chapters 5 and 8 of *Trance-Portation*. You will find a discussion of the right (and wrong) ways to narrate a journey in the same book in Appendix II.

The journeys in this section demonstrate one way to connect with cultural traditions and oracular archetypes and imagery. The first two feature real places with prophetic associations—Delphi and Merlin's Cave at Tintagel. The third will take you to a mythic setting, the Well of Wyrd, from the Germanic tradition. In each of these places, you can ask a question. The fourth journey takes you to an archetypal oracular setting that incorporates images from many cultures and offers you the option not only to question, but also to become the oracle.

One person can narrate for a group, or you can read the text onto a tape for use when working alone. Each journey begins and ends with a standard induction, given in italics in the first journey, which should be read as part of each of the others. Each journey also has a gap in the middle where your question is asked. Allow three to five minutes of silence at this point to let information come through.

Read in a measured tone, avoiding both thrilling narration and a soporific drone. After each instruction, allow a little time for the image to form. Where there are spaces or ellipses, leave extra time. Before you begin, think of a question. If you usually journey with a spirit guide or animal ally, you may call it to go with you as you begin. When you are familiar with the process, use the principles to create journeys that will function for the kind of oracular work you do.

JOURNEY TO DELPHI

As we have seen, the oracle at Delphi was the most respected, though certainly not the only, oracular site in the ancient world. The slopes of Mount Parnassus remain as ruggedly impressive as they were in the days of Plutarch or Pindar, and the gorge below is just as mysterious. But of the complex of temples and treasuries that once adorned them, only the foundations remain. Still, even these are enough to stimulate the imagination, and although we can no longer undertake the physical journey to consult the pythia, in meditation we may find our way to the astral temple created by the memories of the thousands of pilgrims who did make their way to the shrine.

Consider your question carefully before you journey. It is no longer practical to sacrifice a goat, but it might be well to wash your hands and pour out a libation of wine to Apollo before you begin.

Sink down now and be at ease.
Let the solid earth support you, each muscle relax.
Breathe in . . . (eight beats) and out . . . (eight beats)
In . . . and out again . . .
Here you are secure.
All the sounds you hear outside
make it easier to look within.
See now in your mind's eye a place outdoors that you know well.
Look at the ground beneath your feet,
feel its texture, observe the plants that grow there,
note their feel and smell.
Feel the air on your skin,
listen to all the surrounding sounds.
Now, as you look around, you see a path leading away.

Follow it.
To either side grow shrubs that brush against your clothing.
As you move onward, they become taller.
Now they are trees, growing ever closer together and higher
until they arch overhead.
Make your way downward through the tunnel of trees,
through green-scented shadow,
fallen leaves soft beneath your feet.

As you continue, the air grows hot and dry.
The trees are changing, too.
You see small oaks whose pointed leaves rustle in the breeze
and pines whose resinous scent is released by the sun.
Golden light filters through the leaves,
dappling the dusty road.

You pass between a pair of holy cypresses
that point dark green columns at the hot blue sky
and come out on the side of a rugged slope.
To the left, it falls away to the shadows of a deep gorge.
To the right, it rises to frowning heights
textured in brush and ruddy stone.
Below them, a green grove shades the bubbling Castalian spring.
Go to it; bathe your hands and face.
Drink deeply of the clear water.
Be purified of all ill.

Your name has been drawn from the bowl of lots.
The omens are propitious.
Now you can return to the path and seek the sanctuary.
Beyond the precinct wall rise the marble columns and tiled roofs
of treasuries and temples, painted and gilded,
adorned with the fairest statues and most elegant ornaments
that the competing cities of Hellas can provide.
Pass beneath the marble gate and westward along the Sacred Way,
treading stones worn smooth by the passage of many feet.
You hear the murmur of many voices,

the music of stringed instruments, and song.
You smell incense and the rich smoke of burnt offerings.
The precinct is full of people, but all make way for you,
wishing you blessings from the oracle.

Soon the road turns left, up the hill,
then makes a long diagonal up the slope to the right.
Midway, to your left is the great temple of Apollo on its high terrace,
and to your right the great gilded statue of the god.
The road leads past its foundations,
but you turn and mount the broad steps to the terrace.
Here is the altar on which the goat you offered was burned.
Beyond it, the temple itself gleams in the sun.
Above the entrance you read the words "Know thyself."

More steps take you into the cool shade of the sanctuary.
You glimpse statues, the flicker of fire on the sacred hearth,
Then a white-robed priest conducts you around to the right,
along the passage between the columns and the temple wall.
At the western end of the temple there is an inner structure,
a walled and roofed enclosure sunk into the temple floor.
Steps lead down, and you find yourself in a small waiting room,
separated by a curtain from the adyton.

Sit down on the marble bench.
Breathe in . . . There is a hint of sweet scent in the air.
Beyond the curtain you can hear a murmur of voices,
the rustle of cloth, the trickle of water from the spring of Cassotis.
Here is the omphalos stone that is the navel of the world,
and the tripod on which the pythia sits now,
waiting for the god.

A sense of Presence fills the enclosure,
a pressure against your spirit almost too great to bear,
and you know that the god has come.
A sweet scent dizzies you. Your heart beats strongly
as you wait to ask your question.

As the curtains open,
you glimpse a white-draped figure beyond.
The priest comes through, and they close. He asks,
"What do you wish to know?"
Summon the words that across miles and centuries
you have come to say, and wait for the answer . . .

(Allow one to three minutes for meditation.)

The Voice falls silent.
Treasure up the words in your memory . . .
Then follow the priest out of the enclosure and back through the
temple,
where another questioner is waiting to come in.
Your path leads down the steps and away from the temple,
down to the Sacred Way and around,
angling down to the right across the slope of the hill.
Down and around, you pass the treasures
and turn left along the road that leads to the gate.
Follow it through and farther until you pass between the
cypresses,
and find yourself on a dusty path through oaks and pines.
Now the air grows cool once more.

From here you can see the path
that leads through the Wood Between the Worlds.
Follow that path.
Let the green shadows enfold you.
Swiftly and easily, move up the trail
through the tunnel of trees.
Now the trees are farther apart;
you can see the sky above you.
Soon they dwindle to bushes that brush your garments.

The gate to the Place You Know is before you.
Pass through and sink down upon the familiar ground.
Now the earth becomes the floor,

the chair supports you.
The air of this room brushes your skin.
Breathe in and out, and in and out again.
Sigh and stretch; come into your body again.
Open your eyes.
You have returned.

When you are back to ordinary consciousness, write down your impressions. In what way did the answer come to you? Did it make sense? Did you hear words or simply receive information? Was the journey clear, and do you think that you could retrace your steps without the script?

JOURNEY TO MERLIN'S CAVE

In the Celtic traditions, seership is focused not in a place but in a person. Still, figures like Merlin are the focus of an extensive body of legend that includes vivid descriptions of places where one is likely to encounter him. One such place is Tintagel, off the northwest coast of Cornwall, famed as the place where King Arthur was conceived and born (with a little help from Merlin). In the cliffs below the ruins of a medieval castle, we find Merlin's Cave (see the photo in Part One, page 28).

Rather than going in with a question, take your chances and see what the wizard will give you. Begin and end with the induction given in italics on page 168, and continue with the following:

As you descend, the slope grows easier.
The trees are thinning, and now
instead of the wind in the branches
you hear the sound of the sea.
As you emerge from the forest,
you find yourself on a kind of shelf of land
that ends in cliffs above the ocean.
Trees and shrubs cling in the hollows,
but the top is covered with grass,
richly green in the golden light

that glows in the misty air.
A cart track winds toward the fortress
at the edge of the cliff, built of brown stones.

As you near the edge
the hiss and sigh of the sea grows louder.
Breathe deeply of the salt air
and feel the blood sing in your veins.
A brisk wind is blowing from the ocean.
You look over the edge of the cliff—
water swirls like liquid emerald
then disappears in a lacework of spray.
Waves dash against the cliffs, and when they fall away,
you glimpse the dark opening of a cave.
A narrow path winds down the cliff,
dangerous, but it draws you—
the cave draws you,
your need draws you.

Slipping and sliding, you make your way downward.
The tide is out, but the wind is whipping up the sea
and gray clouds are rolling in.
As you pick your way around the narrow beach below the cliffs,
the uncertain light glints on the wet stones.
And now the cave is before you,
dark, deep, sculpted by the sea from gray stone.
Light shafts through the clouds and into the cave,
and what you thought was a rock formation moves.
You recognize the gray robes, flowing beard, twisted staff.
He is as elemental as wind and water, enduring as stone.
Beneath bushy eyebrows, a hawk-bright gaze transfixes you.
Wizard or wildman—what is he?

"What is this a good day for?" you ask,
and he answers you.

(Allow one to three minutes for meditation.)

When he has answered, he points to the sea behind you.
The tide has turned, and the water is coming fast.
You thank him and bow, hurrying back the way you came.
The waves come roaring in, snatching at your ankles;
your face is wet with the damp kiss of the spray,
but you reach the cliff path and climb swiftly,
and turning, look back at the cave.
Within that gaping darkness, a pale light glows.
You catch your breath and remember what the wizard told you.

Then you make your way along the road
until you come to the Wood Between the Worlds
and find shelter from the wind beneath the trees.
Follow that path . . .

Continue with the closing section in italics on page 171.
   When you return, write down what you saw and heard and learned. What or whom did you see? How did your experience differ from other ways of seeking an oracle?

JOURNEY TO VISIT THE NORNS

This journey is based on the cosmology of the Germanic tradition. It will take you to the three Norns at the Well of Wyrd. Begin with the section in italics on page 168 and continue with the following:

At last you see brightness beyond the trees.
As you draw closer, you glimpse a broad plain,
varied with meadow and stream and woodland—
the plain of Midgard that lies within.
A great tree rises in its center.
This is Yggdrasil, axis of all the worlds,
so high its branches brush the heavens,

so wide you can scarcely see around it.
Three great roots plunge through the soil.
Beneath the nearest you see an opening—
the root is polished, and the stones beneath
are worn with the passage of many feet.
Go forward freely, for many have passed this way before.

Pass beneath the root—
a dim, featureless light shows you the way.
You enter from the north.
Mist from Niflheim swirls across your path,
but your way leads onward.
From the center, the shadows of Svartalfheim darken vision,
but you go through them.
Eastward and downward you fare,
past the roots of the moist mountains of Jotunheim,
where the icy rivers flow.
Down and around, down and around you pass,
through the bright, hot air that blows from Muspelheim.

Down and around once more, your way leads westward,
where the waters of the Thunderflood fall in clouds of spray.
There's a rainbow glimmer where Bifrost Bridge arches down.
Here a root of the Tree shelters a deep pool,
Beside it are the judgment seats of the gods and the Well of
Wyrd,
whose sacred waters, poured on that root, forever nourish the
Tree.
Here the Norns sit, to lay down the ørlög of humankind.

Through the veils of spray, you glimpse their faces
as they dip water from the Well and pour it on the roots of the
Tree.
They see you now.

If you dare, address them—
By Well and Tree,
Oh Holy Three,
Sit now, and See . . .
(Incantatory; repeat three times with increasing intensity.)
Ask your question . . .

The waters swirl, glimmering with visions.
Images flicker before you as you hear what they say.

(Allow one to three minutes for meditation.)

The visions fade, the sisters are silent,
the waters of the Well grow still.
Urdh's eyes reflect all that you have been . . .
You meet Verdandi's gaze and understand what you are
becoming . . .
Skuld's smile shows you what can be . . .
You thank them, bow, and turn away.

From the Well, fare up and southward past Muspelheim.
Upward and eastward past Jotunheim you go.
North through the shadows of Svartalfheim and the mists of
Niflheim,
out beneath the root of the tree to the Plain of Midgard.

The Tree grows larger as you approach it,
it is your center, the center of all worlds.

Continue with the closing section in italics on page 171.

Continue with the closing section in italics on page 171.

The visit to the Well of Urdh requires an inner journey, in which a succession of images leads the listener deeper and deeper into a waking dream that opens the mind to messages from within. Do we actually contact the three Norns? Perhaps. Or the images we perceive may be forms created by the mind that enable us to focus on insights that we need. The point is not where the information comes from, but what we choose to do with it.

JOURNEY TO THE ORACLE CAVE

The Oracle Cave is a synthesis of archetypes. Within it, you will find elements common to several traditions. If you are not working in a particular culture, this is the most appropriate journey for you. As in the previous journeys, this path working may be read by a leader or taped by someone who is working alone. Articulate a question to take with you to the cave. If you are working with a group, once the designated seer is seated in the cave and has had a chance to find his or her own answer, others may also ask questions. The induction verses may be chanted or sung (as in the "Veil Song" on page 232).

As with the other meditations, begin by articulating a question. Provide yourself with a veil and pull it over your face when cued. When you have returned, write down your impressions.

Start with the opening induction in italics on page 168 and then continue with the following:

> At last you see a circle of brightness.
> As you draw closer, it resolves into a broad plain,
> varied with meadow and stream and woodland.
> Need compels you onward.
> There are questions that must be answered.
> Where will you find the knowledge you require?
> As you wonder, you hear the sound of water.
> Across the plain, a stream is trickling.
> Follow it, picking your way along the bank toward the hills.
>
> The way is not easy; vines tangle your feet,
> and mud tries to hold them.
> The forest seems ever wilder and darker as you go on.
> Now the ground grows rocky.
> You are making your way upward
> through a gorge that twists and turns

until it disappears into a cavern
guarded by a white cypress tree.

A wind rushes up the gorge, whistling among the stones.
You shiver, but the shadows of the cavern call.
What mystery lies within?
As you approach, the guardian of the cave comes forth to bar
the way,
asking why you have come,
and in your heart, you find the answer.

(Allow one to three minutes for meditation.)

When you have replied, the path grows smooth,
but now you can see
that the stone above the entrance to the cave bears words:
"You who seek wisdom, enter safely.
You who seek your own glory, flee in fear!"

From the cavern, a breath of moist air cools your skin.
But in the shadows you see two points of brightness.
Move toward them . . .

As your eyes adjust, you perceive two torches burning.
Golden light burnishes the arching walls of the cavern,
flickers on the dark waters of the pool that is the source of the
stream.
Beyond it is a tall seat with a step before it.
If it feels right to you, pass around the pool, mount the step,
and sit down.
If this is not the right time, stay where you are.
(Adjust the following instructions to fit your decision.)

Settle into the chair or stand beside the pool.
The solid stone supports you.

A breath of moist air stirs your hair.
Flames glitter on the rippling pool.
Draw the veil over your face,
and light and water become a dim glow.
You hear a chant:

"Behind the Veil you go,
Wisdom's way to show,
Speed onward, seer
Fare without fear,
'til all we need we know. . . ."

Close your eyes and sink into darkness,
Carrying with you only your question.

Wait, listening to the murmur of the water,
The snap of the flame,
the whisper of wind on stone.
In those sounds there are voices.
Wait, as your heart repeats your question.
Wait for the answer . . .

(Allow one to three minutes for meditation.)

Wisdom has come to you.
You will remember what you have learned.
Awareness is returning—
you notice the brush of the veil against your skin,
the cool air, the sounds of wind and fire and stream.
Pull off the veil; look around you.
Light from the entrance to the cave gleams on the pool.
Descend from the chair and move around the water,
thanking the power within.

Pass out into the daylight
and make your way along the gorge, following the stream.
This time the trail seems smooth and easy.
Swiftly you move through the wilderness
until you can see the path
that leads to the Wood Between the Worlds . . .

Continue with the closing section in italics on page 171.

Did you receive an answer to your question? If so, in what form did it come—images, words, a general impression? What was the emotional flavor of your experience?

How did this journey differ from the trip to the Well of Urdh? Reread the text and identify the places where your vision differed from what is written (note: everyone "sees" things differently). What aspects of your own experience or history might account for the changes? Rewrite the text to reflect your own vision.

JOURNEY TO YOUR INNER ORACLE

Using the information and imagery in the preceding sections, write a path working that takes the listener to visit an oracle. This can include a meeting with a historical or mythic oracular figure, as in the journeys to the oracle at Delphi, Merlin, or the three Norns, or you can put the listener (or yourself) into the seat of the oracle, as in the journey to the Oracle Cave. Set the journey in the cultural context with which you are most familiar and to which you respond most deeply.

If you are working with the Celtic tradition, you might consider a wizard's cave, a holy well, or a fairy mound. If you follow the Egyptian gods, the place might be an inner chamber in a temple of Isis or Thoth. If you focus on the Graeco-Roman gods, base your journey on the description of one of the oracular sites in the Mediterranean. If you are Heathen, the journey could be to "sit out" on a grave mound or in the seidhjallr in a chieftain's hall, as described in the sagas.

Another option is to journey in search of an oracular setting and develop your own image based on what you find there.

Analyze the structure of the journeys in this chapter. You will need to create a series of transitional images to move you from the generic opening to the landscape of your journey. Invoke all the senses—texture, scent, temperature. Name a few characteristic plants or trees. Pass from this landscape to the place of the oracle through a gate or other opening. It is useful to include a guardian or signpost that requires you to consent to a deeper level of trance. Furnish the oracular chamber appropriately. In writing the return, be sure to reverse the order in which you encounter each image. Finish with the generic instructions for returning on page 171.

III

WORKING THE RITUAL

You have now been introduced to the skills needed to seek answers for yourself or a few companions, but how does one manage a large public ritual? Oracles can perform in a variety of settings, from the elaborate ritual of Delphi to a chance meeting on the road. Even within the Northern tradition, there are several ways to interpret the evidence. The Three Sisters group uses a minimum of ritual and has questioners form lines to consult seeresses in different corners of the room. In *Hammer of the Gods,* Swain Wodening includes a spae ritual based on a different, and in some ways more faithful, interpretation of the account in the *Saga of Erik the Red,* in which a group of women sing to summon the spirits, and there is no path working. In the form used by Annette Høst, women sing without words as the seeress journeys.

I encourage students to develop their own approaches. Many of those who started in my workshops have developed variations that serve the people well. The "archetypal" or "core oracle" ritual will work for most seers. A culturally embedded form, such as the spae rite, should be used only by those who are working in the tradition from which it comes. That said, since I have the most experience with the spae ritual used by the Seidhjallr group, I'll be analyzing the structure and ritual roles of this form as an example of a ritual that works well for a group with up to sixty people. The full text of the ceremony is included in Chapter IV.

Oracular Seidh (also known as High Seat Seidh) as presently practiced by Seidhjallr is based on the structure described in the *Saga of Erik the Red,* the dialogues between Odin and the Völva in the Elder Edda and on Norse accounts of journeys to the Underworld. As indicated earlier, *seidh* is a general term for several kinds of magic, of which "speaking" answers is only one. *Seidh* is sometimes defined as "messing with minds," and our ritual certainly alters consciousness. I use the term *spae* specifically for the part of the ritual in which the seer answers questions.

After an introduction by the guide that explains the background of the rite and advises the participants on how to best ask questions, the scene is set by songs and invocations to relevant Powers. A path working takes the group to the gate of Helheim. The seer is sung through the gate and deeper into trance, and either answers the questions from Hel or journeys elsewhere. In an alternate form, the journey stops at the Well of Wyrd, and a single seer leaves the path to sit in the cave of the Norns beneath the root of the Worldtree. When all questions have been answered, the seer is brought back through the gate, then all journey back, thank the Powers, and return to consensus reality. Rituals that have been performed regularly over time leave an impression in the Otherworld, and the form used by Seidhjallr now has a weight and momentum of its own.

RITUAL ROLES

In a one-on-one situation, an experienced seer can function without support, but we have found that the larger the group being served, the more important it becomes to divide up the labor. As we have seen, oracles that served large numbers developed a ritual process with specific roles. In one form or another, they include the seer, facilitating clergy (the guide), support staff (one or more warders), and, of course, the people who are asking the questions.

The Seer

Clearly, in an oracular rite, the most visible role is that of the seer. But he or she needs support from others. What is required of those others depends on the level of expertise of the seer and the group for whom the ritual is being performed. Like the Greenland völva, an experienced seer can perform with no more aid than someone to sing the songs and facilitate the questioning, but the less practice the seer has had, the more support he or she will require.

The seer needs to be able to attain a deep trance state without losing focus or being distracted and to develop confidence in his or her ability to do so. However, it is equally necessary to have confidence in one's ability to return from that state and to exercise some control over what happens within it. As a safeguard, we recommend that the seer develop a functional working relationship with a spirit guide, totem, or shamanic ally.

The seer must be able to visualize the journey to the gate of the Underworld and other locations in the Otherworld and to move into a deeper trance state when directed. The journey requires an active exercise of imagination and visualization—the route is known, but the narrator must be able to describe a journey along a predetermined path while filling in the details vividly enough to stimulate vision in the listeners. Once in deep trance, the seer becomes more passive, describing what is perceived in response to the stimulus of the questions. Here, volition is used to seek out and decide how to communicate the vision.

The ability to maintain focus in the secondary trance state (beyond the gate) also seems to be a function of experience. First-time seers generally find three questions more than enough. After several years of practice, our more experienced seers can answer a dozen or more.

A second area of expertise involves cultural background. Everything in the ceremony is intended to move participants into the Germanic sector of the collective unconscious, and while it is not impossible for visions to include contemporary or other cultural material, the seer is most likely to encounter archetypes and images from this area and should be able to recognize and interpret them. In some traditions, for instance, the raven is a harbinger of ill fortune, whereas in Norse mythology the raven is likely to indicate intelligence, knowledge, or the wisdom of Odin. The seer should, therefore, have studied Northern culture enough to feel comfortable with it and to spontaneously express perceptions in a culturally appropriate way.

Finally, the seer should be prepared to help questioners interpret the visions after the session. In some African traditions, prophetic divination is always backed up by reading the cowries for a second opinion. An equivalent in a Norse context would be to offer rune readings on the same questions, with a different person as reader.

The Guide

The guide in an oracular session fills the role ascribed to the master of the house in the account in the *Saga of Erik the Red*. He or she coordinates the ceremony and facilitates the interaction between seer and people. The guide is responsible for setting up the ceremony and orienting the people. In a ceremony that is open to the public, attendees will need a fair amount of instruction in order to participate intelligently.

Before beginning, the guide discusses the structure and teaches the responses/choruses to the group. He or she explains that the introductory purification will help get rid of disruptive energy. The grounding at the end will help people to pull themselves together. The guide should instruct participants to visualize the journey as guided as far as the gate, allowing images to arise without worrying too much about seeing correctly, and emphasize that they *must not go through* (even if they find themselves *seeing* along with the seer). Explain that answers may come directly or as images. Participants should expect to spend time processing the answer, and if there are questions or if the answer contained specific instructions, consider getting a second opinion via the runes or another divination method. The guide emphasizes that anyone who feels disoriented after the ritual should ask for help from one of the crew. When people are linked in trance, they may be unusually vulnerable to the emotions of others.

Other information covered in the introductory talk includes a brief account of the origins of the ritual and guidelines on how to ask questions. The guide should explain that dates and numbers are hard to fix; the best results come from questions in which the asker has an emotional investment, keeps wording short and clear, speaks loudly enough to be heard, comes up to the chair if the seer summons them, but waits for the seer to invite physical contact, if any.

Questions should be focused; additional related questions should be asked separately, after the seer has said, "Would you know more?" To talk to an ancestor or deity, say, "I have a question for X. Can that be answered here?" The guide also reminds people that the information is coming through human filters, and if they think they are being told to do something drastic, they should get a second opinion. If people need follow-up help, the guide should let them know how to contact the team or others who can advise them. The guide also introduces and explains the role of the warders, and emphasizes that anyone who has to leave before the end of the rite must stop at the door and be "talked back" to ordinary consciousness before departing.

The guide should find out approximately how many participants have questions, calculate how many seers will be needed, how many questions to give each, and which seer should go first. The guide usually casts the circle and narrates the journey as well as facilitating the questioning, but the other invocations can be done by any of the team. If the guide is also taking a turn as seer he or she ascends the high seat at the beginning and narrates the journey.

The more experienced the seer, the simpler the role of the guide can become. With seers who are still being trained, however, the guide's role is crucial. In this case, it will be the guide who narrates the journey in and out of the Otherworld as well as putting the seer into second-stage trance. The guide will also need to be more sensitive to the state of the seer and know when it is time to bring him or her back through the gate. If a great deal of emotion has been stirred up by the questions, a seer may have difficulty in finding the way out or be reluctant to leave. In this case, the guide may need the skills to "talk her down" or to journey through the gate him- or herself to bring the wanderer home.

When the number of questioners is great and the trained seers few, the guide should also be prepared to sit in the high seat him- or herself (usually first) and make the transition to guiding others smoothly. Obviously, it is advisable for the guide to be a trained seer, although if the seer is experienced, a good group facilitator can take this role.

In addition to monitoring the condition of the person in the high seat, the guide also has a responsibility to the people who are asking the questions. The questions asked in this kind of session are usually highly important to the asker, and the response may stir up a great deal of emotion. The shared journey seems to place people in a receptive state in which they are likely to be profoundly stirred by the imagery of the visions. However, they will also be more open to the emotions of those around them, and the guide or warders should be ready to deal with any problems.

Skills required by the guide include experience and facility in narrating journeys. If the guide is able to drum well while speaking, a drumbeat can be used to support the path working. She or he should have the ability to maintain rapport with several people at once and to maintain dual levels of consciousness and function in both. For more information on developing these skills see Appendix II of *Trance-Portation*. This is a role requiring discipline, control, and the ability to subordinate one's own needs to those of the group. The guide must be able to think on his or her feet, adjusting timing, content, and wording to circumstances. If physical problems occur in the ceremony (e.g., a piece of equipment has been forgotten, a candle is about to fall over), the guide may have to deal with the situation or delegate the response to a warder without breaking the momentum of the ritual. Afterward, the guide checks on the other participants, both seers and questioners, and makes sure they have grounded and reintegrated, as well as helping questioners to interpret their answers if needed.

Warders

Obviously, the guide's job will be a great deal easier with the assistance of trained warders, essentially assistant guides who focus on the participants and support the seers and questioners during the ceremony. The activities involved in establishing the sacred space can be divided up among the warders, guide, and seers, so that one person handles the purification, another defines the space, others invoke the dwarves and gods, and so on.

One or more people who are strong and active are useful to help the seer up into the high seat and, even more important, to get him or her back down. When the seer has come down, one warder can help with that seer's grounding process while another assists the second seer into the high seat.

Unless the group is small and its members already well known to each other, it is advisable to have one or more additional warders stationed around the periphery and one at the door. Their role is to monitor reactions and to help people enter or leave without disturbing others. They can move to comfort and help ground a questioner if an answer causes distress. If someone needs to leave, the warder does a quick narration of the journey back from the Underworld to bring him or her fully out of trance, and opens a gateway out of the circle.

Warders need to watch for people who may be going too deeply into trance (or have fallen asleep!) and gently bring them back to a light rapport. At the end of the session, warders should check participants as they leave and assist anyone having difficulty coming back to return, ground, and center once more. Warders do not necessarily need to be trained in the oracular process. They do need to be good at staying grounded and helping others to do so, and be sensitive enough to know when someone is in difficulty.

Occasionally someone in the circle may be so troubled that he or she disturbs others, especially those who have opened themselves wide to rapport. In this case, a warder should attempt to set up a shield between that person and the others, and if necessary, assist him or her to leave the circle. For a more extended discussion of the role of a warder, see Appendix II of *Trance-Portation*.

An additional type of warder who is sometimes needed is the "stabilizer," whose job is to help the seer into and out of the high seat and stand behind it while he or she is working. When we work outdoors and the chair is set up on uneven ground, the stabilizer has the very necessary task of holding on and keeping it physically steady. The stabilizer also "watches the back" of the seer, warding off any distracting energy and, if necessary, raises and channels energy into the seer, though he must be careful not to drain his own energy in the process. It is up to the seers to decide whether to have a stabilizer and choose who it should be—usually someone with whom they work well or a close friend or significant other whose energy is compatible with their own.

Questioners

The element that makes the spae ritual different from solo shamanic journeying is the presence of the people with the questions. The Harner technique, in which a shaman journeys to obtain a vision for clients, helps them to interpret it, and teaches them to continue working in this way on their own, occupies a middle position between solo work and the oracle process. Spaecraft allows a seer to use a single journey to see for several people in a way that recreates the culturally supportive environment of a traditional setting. Indeed, only if there are a number of people seeking information of this kind does it make sense to put on such an elaborate ceremony. It might be said, therefore, that next to the seer, the questioners or querents are the most important participants.

Despite the fact that others lead the journey, the role of the questioner should not be a passive one. Increasing the number of people sharing the vision seems to deepen its intensity. Even an experienced journeyer may find the trip more vivid when others are along. The group provides a support network that helps to validate the experience, and the energy and excitement created by group chanting provide extra power to carry the seer into the second level of trance.

Finally, the visions are triggered by the questions themselves. It is the responsibility of questioners to frame the query in a way that will elicit a useful answer, so they should spend some thought on choosing the subject and be specific. Questions should be narrowed down so that a single short vision will provide useful information. They should be serious, and they should be important to the asker.

Interestingly enough, we have found that a vision will sometimes answer both the question that triggered it and a question that someone else in the group was waiting to ask. The visions may stimulate insights in those who have not yet asked a question or did not know they had one. Those not asking questions simply hang out in a comfortable state or do their own spiritual work until it is time to return.

The greater the need of the questioner, the more powerful the vision will be. The process is essentially interactive. Seer and questioners have already been placed in rapport by journeying together; the seer uses his or her skills to reach a level of consciousness in which information and images can be accessed with great efficiency, but the questions evoke the images and validate the seer's belief in his or her skills.

Questioners, therefore, need to stay as focused as possible, to sing enthusiastically when required, and to formulate their questions as simply and clearly as possible. The more open the questioner is to the experience, the more powerful the answer. The answer may be something the questioner has been told before or advice that could be communicated just as well in a less elaborate setting, but if the information is communicated when both parties are in an altered state, it has more impact. The visions can have great power, and even ordinary information conveyed in trance may acquire profound significance. In any case, the questioner is more likely to remember and understand advice received in this way.

RITUAL STRUCTURE

The basic elements in a ritual are also consistent across time and tradition—getting ready, invoking the Powers, helping the seer to move into trance, facilitating the questions, and getting everyone back to normal afterward.

Preparation

Some of the most important parts of the ritual come before it even begins. The team should gather before the ritual to establish rapport and confirm who is performing each role (including the invocations and how the warders will cover the area). When they arrive at the ritual site (if different), they will set up the high seat, candles, etc., and do any cleansing or banishing needed to dispel influences from previous use of the room (especially important at a large and busy conference such as Pantheacon).

Setting the Stage

In religions with a permanently dedicated meeting space, the simple act of walking into the temple cues participants to shift to an appropriate state of consciousness. But even Christian ceremonies usually begin with prayers that focus participants on the business at hand. This is even more essential when we have to integrate people from varied backgrounds into a specific cultural context and persuade them that the hotel function space or living room is sacred ground.

The first step is purification, which banishes tensions and preoccupations that would prevent us from focusing on the work at hand. One team member circles the room, using a sprig of greenery to sprinkle participants and the seidh seat, etc., with water from a bowl. Carrying a candle around the room or smudging with herbs also achieves this purpose, but using water avoids problems with smoke alarms. The guide or householder defines the space to be used for the ceremony, using whatever other format is customary for the group. Next, the guide or another member of the team may orient and balance the group by honoring the directions and the local nature spirits. In the Seidhjallr version, we honor the four dwarves who in Norse lore hold up the four corners of the world.

Finally, we invoke Odin and Freyja, the deities associated with seidh and spirit journeying, along with the ancestors and Hella, to whose home we are traveling. With each step, the group moves deeper into the world of Norse myth. By the time the journeying begins, everyone should be caught up by the momentum of the ceremony. Singing helps to create the mood, involve the participants, and raise energy.

In most traditions, the gods were invoked before performing divination, and doing so has an important psychological function. Establishing sacred space provides a transitional period in which the participants can release the preoccupations of the day and their identities in the modern world and move into the world of Nordic myth. It also defines the ritual area.

Transition

The second part of the ritual helps participants shift to a state of consciousness in which answers can be obtained and understood. It begins with a formal prayer to the three Norns for truth and clarity, followed by the path working that takes the group to the gates of Hel.

The journey is narrated by the guide or the first seer, who may also be drumming. It always follows the same general outline, but each narrator describes it differently. The induction begins with the standard opening used for the journeys in Chapter II of Part Two. The Wood Between the Worlds is the barrier between the real world and Midgard, which is the Middle World, the nonordinary version of our normal plane of existence. In its center rises Yggdrasil, the Worldtree. From this point, the journey follows the traditional Norse map of the Nine Worlds to the gate to Hel, where all except the seers will wait during the questioning. The whole group is carried along on the journey. Each participant interprets the narration through his or her own symbol system, but everyone arrives at the same goal. This shared journey recreates the common cultural context of a traditional society. It also places the entire group in a rapport that facilitates the divination.

The journey concludes at the gate of the Underworld. At this point, the guide requires the seer to formally consent to go more deeply into trance to answer questions. The seer ascends the seidhjallr and is sent off with a quotation from *Vafthruthnismál*. The energy to move the seer into second-stage trance is provided by the singing of the guide and questioners. The music, based on a Norwegian folk song, carries the seer as he or she visualizes going through the gateway of the Underworld.

Perhaps because the ancestors are part of the primal earth and thus connected to its spirits, we have found that Helheim is the easiest place from which to seek a wide variety of answers; however, some seers prefer to journey to the Well of Wyrd or a location such as Odin's Seat of Seeing.

Spae

The guide continues to sing and drum, observing the seer carefully until changes in his or her energy indicate a deeper state of trance. Most seers hide their faces with a veil or hood, and their eyes are closed. At this point, the guide waits for a few minutes to allow the seer to settle firmly in. The guide then summons the seer to attention with a formal spell that ends with a request to describe what he or she sees and whether he or she can answer questions here. This serves to "prime the pump" and accustom the seer to responding.

The guide now turns to the group and asks who has a question. When someone raises his hand, the guide indicates that he should speak, then cues the seer to answer with the words Odin used to compel an answer from the Völva in the *Dream of Baldr*. The seer signals the end of an answer with some variant of "This you know, would you know more?" If time allows, the questioner may ask for further information; otherwise, he says thank you to indicate acceptance of the answer, and the seer sinks back into the neutral state.

The role of the guide is to act as intermediary between the other participants, still in a light trance, and the seer, and facilitate the questioning. The guide signals questioners to begin and indicates the end of a sequence. He or she also maintains rapport with the seer. If there are more questions than the first seer can handle, a second, and, if required, a third seer, is put up into the high seat, and the sequence from the singing onward is repeated. The guide must evaluate the state of the seer in the high seat and decide when to bring him or her out of trance. As a seer approaches his or her previous limit, the guide should ask how he or she is doing. If the seer seems fatigued or the clarity of the answers is fading, the guide should bring him or her out of trance.

In the Viking Age, those who wished to speak with the dead usually "sat out" on the grave mound, but the spiritualist movement has imprinted the concept of the séance on our culture. Participants in a spae rite may have questions involving the dead, or there may be times when a seer senses spirits who are eager to communicate. Given that we are invading the realm of the ancestors for this work, it seems only just that they should be allowed to have their say. The seer may hear and transmit the message or, in some cases, allow the spirit to speak through him or her. This kind of communication, however, should be handled carefully, and special attention should be paid to bringing the seer back to ordinary consciousness. The same goes for questions addressed to gods. The guide can request that questions for specific deities be saved for the seers who work with them, or request people to phrase questions indirectly: "Can you ask Odin what he wants me to do with my life?" instead of "What does Odin want?" In most cases, the seer will have to journey to a different part of the Otherworld in order to speak with a deity.

Returning to the World

When questions, time, or the energy of the seer runs out, the guide brings the seer back from deep trance through the gate, but offers him or her the option of remaining in the seidhjallr for the journey home. The guide narrates the return journey in reverse order from the way people came. At the end of the narration, there is another song, which gives people a little more time to reconnect with their bodies. All those Powers that were invoked are thanked, and the space is returned to ordinary use.

The closing ritual recapitulates the actions of the opening in reverse order, assisting all participants to make an orderly transition back to normal reality. Warders offer water or a little salt to make sure that everyone has, in fact, shifted consciousness. Kosher or rock salt gives a tactile as well as taste stimulus. Sour salt (citric acid crystals) is even more effective. We always try to have food and drink available afterward to replace expended energy. The social atmosphere of sharing food also provides a supportive environment in which people can debrief and discuss their answers.

PRODUCTION VALUES

The most important requirements for spaecraft are the participants. The only equipment really needed to journey is the mind. However, when one is working with a group, a certain amount of dramatic technique

THE WAY OF THE ORACLE

increases effectiveness. In addition to researching the process itself, we have tried to include elements from the culture from which it comes. Members of the team wear traditional garments. Appropriate verses are embroidered in runes on ceremonial shawls or tooled into the leather of belts. As those who work the Renaissance Pleasure Faire and other period-themed events have found, putting on the clothes of another time and place is the first step in time travel.

If candles are substituted for electric lighting, little more is required to support the illusion that one has reached another century. Electric candles can serve when hotel regulations forbid open flame. Seidhjallr has performed this rite outdoors in mist or in moonlight, in an underground bunker, in a tent in the rain, in hotel function rooms, and in the living rooms of private homes.

The single item that identifies the oracle most clearly is the special chair. The Delphic oracle has her tripod; the Greenland völva, her

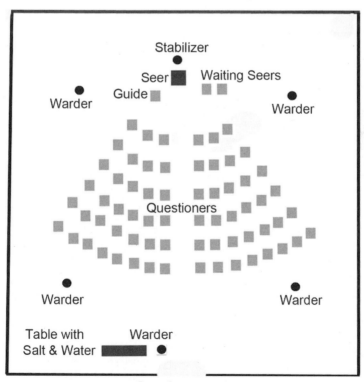

Setup for a spae rite

seidhjallr. The seat from which the seer will speak should be stable, provide good back support, and look imposing. An antique carved chair or an ordinary chair that has been covered with a pretty cloth will do, especially if it can be elevated on a pallet or dais. A sturdy bar chair can also be used. My group possesses a massive elevated chair that can be taken apart for transport (see the photos on pages 34, 43, and 44 in Part One), but high seats have been improvised from chairs covered with cloth. It is essential that the chair be stable. On uneven ground outdoors, you may need to assign someone to hold it steady.

Other requirements include a central spot from which the seer can be seen and heard and places where people can sit comfortably for an extended period. The person guiding the rite will need a seat as well. A typical layout is shown on the previous page.

IV

APPLICATIONS

We have covered the history, theory, and skills involved in the work of the oracle. In this section, let's look at some examples of how they can be put into practice. All of these are rituals that I and/or my group have presented. To work alone requires self-knowledge, self-discipline, strength, and the ability to align oneself with the positive currents of the universe. Community oracles work together to see for each other and pool their energy to work for the community. Individual members of such a group do not all have to be equally good at all aspects of the work.

All of the large-group rituals have the same basic structure and, in places where the procedure is independent of culture, the same or similar words. By comparing elements, you can identify the essence and use that information to build your own rituals.

IMPROMPTU ORACLE

Before getting into the large group form of oracle work, let's look at the simplest form of oracular practice, in which a seer drops into trance and answers a question. An impromptu oracle can also *see* for herself. The "three Rs" of the process are *readiness, reception,* and *response.*

> **Readiness.** First, you need a safe space. Seek a spot where you are unlikely to be interrupted; ward yourself with an energy circle or psychic shield, and invoke your helping spirits or allies to stand guard. If you are answering for another person, he or she can also act as warder.

> **Reception.** The next step is to articulate the question. Repeat it mentally, or tell the person you are *seeing* for to state what he needs to know. This is the stimulus that cues you to close your eyes, count

your breathing, and follow the sequence that cues you to shift consciousness. Allow yourself to sink into a receptive state and clear the channels, releasing all thoughts except the question. Mentally repeating a mantra or chant to which you have been trained to respond is also effective.

Response. When you have attained the receptive state, open your awareness to information. When you get a fix on the answer, respond to the questioner aloud, or shift consciousness, return to ordinary awareness, and write down or tell the questioner what you learned. This can be followed by some discussion in which you explore interpretations.

Here is one example. I was sitting in a pleasant courtyard outside a coffee shop, worrying, as one often does, about finances. It seemed like a good day to ask a question, so I mentally surrounded myself with a bubble of protecting energy and invoked a circle of wolves to guard me, waiting until I could feel the shift in the surrounding energy before continuing. Then I articulated the question, "Where can I find resources for prosperity?"

I relaxed, balanced, closed my eyes, and began to count and slow my breathing, clearing my mind until all I could "see" was a blank of warm, bright color behind my eyelids. Then I mentally "sang" the passage song we use in oracular seidh and felt the familiar shift and dip as I moved into deeper trance.

In my mind, I saw a path through woods that led to an open field. Something like this has often been a setting for a vision that will answer the question, but all I could see was the field. I wondered if maybe this *was* the vision, and then I realized that someone was digging there, weeding, tilling the soil. Crows were busy around the disturbed ground, snapping up bugs.

As soon as this was clear, the interpretation also began to come to me, and I realized that I already had the resources. The fertile field held ideas and previous work. I needed to cultivate and develop what I already had. The process would reveal useful/saleable bits and pieces.

I let the vision fade and return to the blank color of the sun shining through my closed eyelids, then I quickened my breathing and refocused my awareness on the sounds around me. When I was fully conscious, I opened my eyes, thanked and dismissed my guards, and took down my circle. I completed the process by writing down the results and turning them into a couplet.

Rich soil, tangled weeds,
Till the earth, release the seeds.

CORE ORACLE RITE

Building on the same imagery we used in the Journey to the Oracle Cave on page 176, this ritual elaborates and develops it for use with a general audience. It is not essential to include the chants, but they do help to raise energy and involve the participants. If you are not working in a specific culturally based tradition, this form, or something like it, is the one you should use. You will observe that some of the lines are repeated in other rituals—if you are working in more than one context, it is easier to retain some of the same cues.

Props: bowl of water, a staff or gilded branch representing the "golden bough," candle, impressive chair, veil, salt in dish, glass of water.

Preparation

Before the ritual, the guide explains the process, instructs the people on how to ask their questions, and introduces the songs.

Purification

The guide or another team member carries the bowl counterclockwise around the circle, sprinkling participants with water while saying:

Water from the sacred spring,
Banish ill and blessings bring.

Sacred Space

Go clockwise around the circle with your staff or a gilded branch representing the talisman that got Aeneas safely through the Underworld. As you do, say:

Sunwise ward the circle round,
By golden bough the way's unwound.

Safely come and safely go
'til everything we need we know.

Invocations to the quarters/elements may be added here.

Invocations and Offerings

To the Fates (the Holy Three):

Sacred sisters, now we summon
To foresee what fate has fashioned—
What has been, what is being, and becoming.
Be there truth in our seeing, truth in our saying,
Understanding in the ears that hear!
Bestowers of blessings, from our words breed good fortune!
Accept now our offering.

Light a candle or pour out some wine.

All sing "Hallowed Well of Wisdom" (see page 231). Invocations to specific gods and goddesses, such as Hermes, may be added here.

Path Working

This is essentially the same journey used throughout Chapter II of Part Two. Begin with the standard journey opening that appeared in the Journey to Delphi in that chapter (see the italicized passages on page 169). After passing through the tunnel of trees, continue with the following:

Presently you come out onto a broad plain,
varied with meadow and stream and woodland.
It is need that compels you onward—
there are questions that must be answered
Where will you find the knowledge you require?

As you wonder, you hear the sound of water.
Across the plain, a stream is trickling.
You start to follow it,
picking your way along the bank toward the hills.
The way is not easy; vines tangle your feet

and mud tries to hold them.
The forest seems ever wilder and darker as you go on.

Now the ground grows rocky.
You are making your way upward
through a gorge that twists and turns,
until it ends in a cavern beside a white cypress tree.
A wind rushes up the gorge, whistling among the stones.
You shiver, but the shadows of the cavern call you.
What mystery lies within?
As you approach, the guardian of the cave comes forth to bar
the way,
asking why you have come here,
and in your heart, you find the answer.

When you have replied, the path grows smooth,
but now you can see
that the stone above the entrance to the cave bears words:
"You who seek wisdom, enter safely.
You who seek your own glory, flee in fear!"

From the cavern comes a cool breath of air,
damp with the scent of water.
But in the shadows you see the flicker of a fire
Flaming torches are reflected in the dark waters of a pool.

You stop, for this is the Cave of the Oracle,
and one only can enter here.

The Oracle

Guide: Who will dare the waiting darkness?
Who will seek the cavern and pass between the fires?
Who will sit at the well and speak the will of Fate?

Seer: I will.

Guide: Take your place upon the sacred seat;
draw the Veil of Vision between yourself and the world.

The seer is seated and veiled.

Guide: The fire illuminates you;
the spring murmurs secrets.
As you wait for the questions, all wisdom is yours.

All sing "Veil Song" (see page 232). Allow a short period for the seer to sink into trance.

Guide: [Magical name] am I, through worlds have I wandered,
seeking the seer whom now I summon.
By blood and bone, by stock and stone,
by time and tide, by waters wide,
by breath and breeze, by fire that frees,
come to my summoning.
[Magical name] canst thou hear me
from depths of darkness where thou art dreaming?

The seer responds.

Guide: Say then, seer, what dost thou see?

The seer responds.

Guide—to the people: Within the cave the seer now waits.
Who among you has a question?

The guide identifies and motions to a first querent to speak. When the question has been asked, the guide continues:

Say then, seer, till said thou hast,
answer the asker, till all he (or she) knows.

The seer answers. When he or she has finished, he or she says, "I see no more."

Guide: Well hast thou asked, and well been answered.
Is there another who has a question?

The questions continue until all questions have been asked or it is time for another seer to sit. Bring back the seer by saying something like:

> The visions fade; the questions are answered.
> You who have carried the power, release it now.
> Leave well and tree behind you; pass between the fires.
> Emerge from the cavern into the light.
> The veil falls away. You are yourself again.
> (The veil is lifted.)
> [Name], return to stand with the people.

If additional seers are serving, assist the first seer to rise, with whatever additional coaxing is needed, and sit down with the people. Give him or her a little water, etc. Repeat the process with the other seers. Bring in a new seer by returning to "The Oracle" portion of the ritual and repeating the procedure.

Return

When the last seer has left the well, lead the group back to consensus reality by narrating the journey in reverse order:

> We turn from the cavern, remembering what we have learned,
> and make our way along the gorge, following the stream.
> This time the path seems smooth and easy.
> Swiftly we make our way through the wilderness
> until we can see the path
> that leads to the Wood Between the Worlds.

Continue with the italicized ending of the path working in the Journey to Delphi on pages 171 to 172. To help ground, all sing "This We Know" (see page 233).

Thanks and Farewells

Give thanks to any gods and/or goddesses on whom you have called and then to the Fates.

To the Fates (the Holy Three):
Now we salute the sacred sisters,

Holy Three, who brought us blessings
And spun the thread with strands of wisdom,
Sink down to our depths once more as we thank you—
Hail and farewell!

All: Hail and farewell!

If the quarters/elements were invoked, they should be dismissed here.

Open Circle

Round about I walk the way,
Sacred circle, fade away,
This place to all good use returned,
leave us with the lore we've learned!

Offer salt or water to help people ground.

THREE NORNS SPAE

This form was originally developed as a training ritual for use at workshops. Putting three people into trance together lessens the pressure on each one and decreases performance anxiety. Matching new people with those who are more experienced allows the former to pick up the skill through rapport, and by seating several teams one after another, we can give more people a taste of what it is like to do the work. The advantage of having three seers is that they can pass the answer back and forth, developing it and stimulating each other to see further. The disadvantage is that getting three perspectives on a question takes three times as long, so it is most useful when there are a limited number of questioners.

The imagery and references come from the Germanic tradition; however, the rite could be easily adapted to core oracle format by identifying the seers with the Fates and placing three seats in the Oracle Cave. The Norns are, of course, Urdh, Verdandi, and Skuld. Some teams divide up their answers, with one covering the past, one the present, and one the (probable) future. But Germanic tradition also includes lesser norns, who watch over individuals and families. It is wiser for seers to identify themselves with these rather than attempting to carry the weight of the Big Three.

Props: cloth to cover chairs, long veil, staff, bowl for water, pitcher of water, glasses, salt.

Preparation

The guide explains that the group will be journeying to the Well of Wyrd (aka, the Well of Urdh). The seers will sit by the pool, and others will question. The seers sit together, facing the others. They should be close enough so that their shoulders are touching, or they can hold hands. Cover all three with a single veil.

Purification

Go around the circle, sprinkling all participants with water while saying:

> With water from the Well of Wyrd
> All ill that has been, all ill that is becoming,
> All ill that shall be,
> is banished away.

Sacred Space

The guide moves clockwise around the circle, saying:

> Sunwise I walk the way of wonder.
> With sacred staff the worlds I sunder.
> As I walk the circle round,
> by wit and will may it be bound.

Invocation of the Norns

> Sacred sisters, now we summon
> to foresee what fate has fashioned—
> what has been, what is being and becoming.
> Be there truth in our seeing, truth in our saying,
> understanding in the ears that hear!
> Bestowers of blessings, from our words breed good fortune!

All sing "Spindle Song" (see page 234).

Path Working

Use the standard journey beginning used in the Journey to Delphi in Part Two, Chapter II (see the italicized passages on pages 168 to 169). After passing through the tunnel of trees, continue with the following:

> At last you see a circle of brightness.
> As you draw closer, you glimpse a broad plain,
> varied with meadow and stream and woodland—
> the plane of Midgard that lies within.
> A great tree rises in its center.
> This is Yggdrasil, axis of all the worlds,
> so high its branches brush the heavens,
> so wide you can scarcely see around it.
> Three great roots plunge through the soil.
> Beneath the nearest you see an opening—
> the root is polished and the stones beneath it
> worn by the passage of many feet.
> Go forward freely, for many have passed this way before.
>
> Bend beneath the root—
> a dim, featureless light shows you the way.
> Mist swirls across your path from Niflheim,
> but your way leads onward.
> The shadows of Svartalfheim darken vision,
> but you go through them.
> Eastward and downward you go,
> past the roots of the moist mountains of Jotunheim,
> where the icy rivers flow.
> Down and around, down and around you pass,
> through the bright, hot air that blows from Muspelheim.
> Down and around once more, your way leads westward.
>
> The waters of the Thunderflood fall in clouds of spray
> with a rainbow glimmer where Bifrost Bridge arches down.
> A root of the Tree shelters a deep pool
> surrounded by the judgment seats of the gods.

Here is the Well of Wyrd, whose sacred waters,
poured on that root, forever nourish the Tree.
Here the Norns sit, to see and say the *ørlög* of humankind.

The Oracle

Guide—to the seers: [Name], [Name], and [Name], look now at the Tree.
Beneath its root the Well is waiting.
Will you look into it, to see for the people?

The seers agree.

Sink down, take your sibling's hand.

The Tree protects you;

the Well murmurs secrets.
All wisdom is yours as you wait for the questions to come.

Say the following incantation three times with increasing intensity:

By Well and Tree,
Oh Holy Three,
Sit now, and See.

All sing "Holy Three" (see page 235).

Guide—to the people: Beside the Well the Norns now wait.
Who among you has a question?

The guide identifies and motions to a first querent to speak. When the question has been asked, the guide continues:

Norns, now give answer, till said ye have,
answer the asker, till all he (she) knows.
Look into the Well and seek vision there.

The first seer to get an image/information begins to speak. When he or she finishes, he or she asks, "Sister/Sibling, what do you see?" The next speaks, and then the third. When the third has finished, he or she asks, "Sisters/siblings, do you see more?" and there may be one or more rounds. Deferring to and encouraging each other, the three seers discuss and answer the question. As each seer senses the vision is finished, he or she says, "I see no more."

When all three have said "I see no more," the guide asks for another question.

> **Guide—to the people:** Well hast thou asked, and well been answered.
>
> Is there another who has a question?

The guide repeats the request for questions until all questions have been asked or it is time for another team to sit. Bring back the trio of seers by saying something like:

> The visions fade; the questions are answered.
> You who have carried the power, let it pass.
> The veil falls away, you are yourselves again.

Assistants lift the veil.

> [Name], [Name], [Name], return to stand with the people.

If additional teams are serving, assist the first seer to rise, with whatever additional coaxing is needed, and sit down with the people. Give him or her a little water, etc. Repeat the process with the other seers. Bring in the new trio by returning to "The Oracle" and repeating the procedure.

Return

When the last trio has answered questions and left the well, lead the entire group back to consensus reality by narrating the journey in reverse order:

> From the Well, up and southward past Muspelheim.
> Upward and eastward past Jotunheim.
> North through the shadows of Svartalfheim and the mists of Niflheim.
> Out beneath the root of the Tree to the Plain of Midgard.
> The Tree grows larger as you approach it.
> It is your center, the center of all worlds.

From here, bring participants back to consensus consciousness using the standard closing induction introduced in the Journey to Delphi in Part Two, Chapter II (see the italicized text on pages 171 to 172).

To help ground, all sing "This We Know," on page 233.

Assist the first seer to rise, with whatever additional coaxing is needed, and sit down with the people. Give him or her a little water, etc. Repeat the process with the other seers.

Thanks and Farewells

Guide: Now we salute the sacred sisters,
the Holy Three, who brought us blessings
from the Well with words of wisdom.
Sink down to our depths once more as we thank you—
hail and farewell!

All: Hail and farewell!

Open the Circle

The guide bears the staff counterclockwise around the circle with the words,

Round about and back again,
Sacred circle be undone,
This place to all good use returned,
leave us with the lore we've learned!

AN ORACLE OF APOLLO

The format of this ritual is different, as the oracle rite has been fitted into the ritual structure developed by Pürokanthos for the Thiasos Olympikos, a Hellenic tradition. For more about their work and scripts for their other rituals, see *home.pon.net/rhinoceroslodge/thiasos.htm*.

The oracular sequence is inspired by what we know of the Delphic and other Classical Greek oracles. The ritual roles include the thespode, a priest or priestess who transmits words to and from the oracle and is essentially the same as the guide; the oracle, who channels Apollo; and an assisting priest or priestess. These roles can be taken either by women or men. Note that in the Hellenic tradition, the sacred direction is counterclockwise.

This rite requires rather a lot of props, which are listed before the script. Ideally, one would have a sacred hearth, but if a fireplace is not available, a large bowl or tray with many votive lights may be used. A curtain or screen to hide the oracle until time for the Mantike is desirable. The practice of having the questions written down and read to the oracle by the thespode was originally intended to guarantee that the oracle could not identify the questioner. If this is not a concern, the questions can be spoken aloud in the order determined by the lots.

Sacra and tools: white altar cloth and candles, image of Apollon, large bowl, pitcher of water, towel, bowl of water, branch of laurel or other greenery, fireplace or metal dish with several votives, small bowl of uncooked barley, bottle opener, sweet red wine, bottle of springwater, bread on a platter, krater (mixing bowl) and chalice, basket of lots (numbered pottery shards), pad of paper and pencils, "tripod" stool (a bar stool or other elevated seat), a curtain or screen (if possible), matches, spray of dry laurel leaves or incense and holder or metal bowl on trivet, bag or basket for offerings.

The oracle, thespode, and priest(ess) should all wear white. The oracle will also need a white veil.

Preparation

After the people have gathered, the assisting priest(ess) leads them out to form up for the procession. When they have left the sanctuary, the thespode formally asks if the oracle is willing to be a voice for the god and, when he or she agrees, seats him or her on the stool, on which the seer sits completely veiled. If possible, place a curtain or screen between the oracle and the ritual area. The oracle can use the time during the ritual to meditate and move into trance.

Meanwhile, the assisting priest(ess) distributes the sacra (the bowl of barley, knife, incense, krater, bottle of water, bottle of wine, and spray of dry laurel leaves) to participants to carry. He or she distributes paper and pencils so that people can write their questions. When everyone is ready, the door is opened, and the thespode welcomes them.

> **Thespode:** From many lands the seekers of the shrine
> have come, and you the latest among many,
> I welcome you. May your search be blessed;
> may Apollon's radiance illuminate your souls.
> Now we serve the god and praise him—
> attend, and pray, and hope, therefore,
> that the lord of light himself may show us his glory!
> Listen to the dawn-hymn to Apollon that was written by Euripides.

> **Assisting Priest(ess):** See, the sun! His chariot-light
> O'er the earth already speeds,
> while before his fiery steeds
> fly the stars into the vasty night.
> See Parnassus' summits bright,
> pathless peaks, by daybreak lit,
> which to the wide world welcome it!
> Smoke of the unshowered frankincense
> soars to Phoebus' roof divine;
> the priestess waits Apollo's sign.
> On the tripod waits Apollo,
> there to hear his voice and follow
> forth in public chant his secret sense.
> Go, his Delphian servants, ye
> to the silver eddies of Castaly
> and bathe yourselves, and come again,
> clean and made holy, to the fane.
> Guard your speech, that never word
> on your noble lips be heard
> to mar their purpose, who resort
> for question to this sacred court.
> I the while the task fulfill
> which is mine from childhood still,
> with laurel-bough in mystic tie
> the portal here to purify.

The priest(ess) takes the basin and laurel branch and uses them to sprinkle water to purify the ritual area, then returns to the foyer.

The Ritual

The assisting priest(ess) leads the people to the *temenos,* or sacred precinct, containing the altar of sacrifice. He or she stops at the entrance to the temenos and assists each person to perform the *khernips,* or hand washing, directing them to silently move counterclockwise around the altar to find a place in the semicircle of chairs. When all are seated, the thespode cries out—

> **Thespode:** *Hekas, o hekas, este bebeloi!*
> Let all that is profane be far from here!
> We are here to honor the gods and goddesses.

The thespode lights the candles on the altar.

The assisting priest(ess) invites the person carrying the barley to move counterclockwise to the altar table, open and place the box there, toss a few grains into the fire or bowl of candles, and return counterclockwise around the circle. Each subsequent person follows suit. The libation bearers move to either side of the thespode and simultaneously pour the wine and water into the krater so that it mixes there.

> **Thespode:** Behold the Waters of Life!
> Hestia, Thine is always the first and the last.

Some of the mixture in the cup is sprinkled on the fire, then the cup is passed around counterclockwise, each person taking a sip in honor of Hestia, or touching a drop to his or her forehead, and repeating the above formula. The priest(ess) takes a last sip, and the remaining liquid is poured out on the hearth or platter of candles.

> **Assisting Priest(ess):** Hear, O people, how Callimachus sang to the god!

> How Apollon's laurel sapling shakes!
> How the whole temple shakes! Away, away with the wicked!
> It must be Phoebus kicking at the door with his fair foot.
> Do you not see? The Delian palm nods gently,

All of a sudden; the swan sings beautifully in the air.
Bolts of the doors, thrust yourselves back.
Keys—open the doors! For the god is no longer far away.
So, young men, prepare yourselves for singing and dancing.
Apollon appears not to all, only to the good.
Be silent and hear the song of Apollon's glory.
Even the sea is silent, for bards celebrate
the cithara and bow, weapons of Lycoreian Phoebus.
Golden is Apollon's mantle and golden its clasp,
as are his lyre and Lyctian bow and quiver;
golden are his sandals, for Apollon is rich in gold.
Always fair, always young!
Never do traces of down touch his blooming cheeks.
His hair drips fragrant oils to the ground,
but streaming from the locks of Apollon is not fat but panacea.
In the city where these dewdrops fall to earth, all things are
secure.
None is so versatile in skill as Apollon.
He watches over the archer; he watches over the bard;
Phoebus's are both the bow and the song.
His are the prophets and prophetesses;
from Phoebus physicians learn the skill of postponing death.
Men who plan cities are followers of Phoebus,
for Phoebus rejoices in the founding of cities,
and Phoebus himself lays the foundations.
The chorus which sings to Apollon with its heart he will honor.
He has the power; he sits on the right hand of Zeus.
Neither will the chorus sing of Apollon for only one day;
he is worthy of many hymns.
Who would not readily sing of Apollon?

The libation bearers again mix water and wine. The thespode offers up the cup and says, "Apollon, this *sponde* is for You, in the hope that You will join us here today."

The thespode sprinkles some of the mixture on the fire, then passes the cup counterclockwise. When the libation returns, he or she takes a last sip, and the remaining liquid is poured out on the hearth or platter of candles.

The thespode takes the bread and stabs it, and the women in the group perform the ullulation, a ritual cry of mourning. Those who have brought canned food to donate to the needy bring it forward. The thespode touches each thing to be offered with the sacrificial knife. Each one who is making an offering may say, as it is offered, "Accept and delight in my offering."

When all offerings have been made, the thespode says, "Accept and delight in our offerings."

> **Thespode or Priest(ess):** Behold the greatness of the god, thus do we honor him!
> Let us therefore seek his blessing now!
> As I sing to invoke him, you shall be my chorus,
> listen to the words and to the tune;
> when I sing it, then you shall sing with me,
> echoing the refrain of the soaring song!

All sing "Paean" (see page 236).

Everyone visualizes Apollon and anticipates the coming of the god. The music also serves as an invocation of Apollo. As it is sung, the waiting oracle sinks into a deeper trance.

The Mantike

The assisting priest(ess) passes around the bowl of numbered lots. Each questioner takes one. The priest(ess) lights the dry laurel at the altar flame, sets it in the metal bowl, and fans smoke toward the oracle. He or she then sets the bowl on a trivet before the stool. The thespode calls on the god, asking if he will speak through the oracle. The thespode and oracle should agree ahead of time on an invocation or cue to which the oracle will respond, such as breathing the smoke of the incense or burning laurel leaves. When the thespode receives a positive answer, he or she opens the curtain or moves the screen (if any) to reveal the oracle.

> **Thespode:** The god is in his holy temple. His voice awaits. Who now would ask a question?

The querent who drew the lot numbered one gives his or her written question to the assisting priest(ess) to give to the thespode, who goes to the oracle and reads it, or the question may be spoken aloud. The oracle replies. The thespode repeats or interprets the answer if needed. When all have asked their questions, the thespode thanks the god and asks him to release the oracle. The assisting priest(ess) attends to the oracle while the thespode finishes leading the ritual.

Thanksgiving

If all the liquid in the krater has been used, the libation bearers mix wine and water again, and the priest(ess) ladles it into the cup. Some of the mixture in the cup is sprinkled on the fire, then the cup is passed around counterclockwise, each person taking a sip in offering to Apollon or touching a drop to his or her forehead in offering and saying, "Apollon, we thank You."

The thespode takes a last sip, and the remaining liquid is poured out onto the hearth. If necessary, the libation bearers mix wine and water one final time.

> **Thespode:** Hestia, Thine is always the first and the last.

The cup is passed around counterclockwise, each person taking a sip in honor of Hestia or touching a drop to his or her forehead in offering and saying, "Hestia, we thank You."

The thespode takes a last sip, and the remaining part is poured out on the bowl.

> **Thespode:** So be it!

The assisting priest(ess) assists the oracle to descend from the stool and takes him or her to the robing room. The thespode remains with the participants, who are welcome to help finish off the wine.

ORACULAR SEIDH (SPAE)

This is the ritual with which my group began. It has been expanded and refined over the years. It was originally designed for use with large groups at festivals and works well with up to sixty people. If the numbers are larger, some will be outside the energy field of the seer, and the rite will lose focus. If there are more than forty or so questions, the guide and the rest of the supporting team will be exhausted, even if the seers, who are in trance, are still fine. My experience has been that the larger the group, the more structured the ritual needs to be to focus and maintain the energy.

The same ritual can be used to do spae at the Well of Urdh, with the change that the journey stops at the well (as in the Three Norns ritual), and as in that ritual, Hella and the ancestors are not invoked. The lines that are underlined should be memorized and used exactly, as they are cues to which the seers are trained to respond.

Props: seidhjallr (note: a high seat may be improvised by covering a chair with a fancy cloth), candles, drum (optional), bowl of water and sprig of greenery, rock salt.

The guide's seat is positioned below the high seat and to one side with a small table to hold the blessing bowl, the drinking horn or glass of water, the script book, the salt, and a candle. If the guide is not also the drummer, the drummer should have a seat facing the guide. Seats for the additional seers are set to either side of the high seat.

Turn lights low or out; light with more candles.

I. Establishing Sacred Space

Purification

One of the team circles the room with a bowl of water and a sprig of greenery, which he or she uses to sprinkle everyone and everything, including the high seat. While doing so, he or she chants:

> With water from the Well of Wyrd
> all ill that has been,
> all ill that is becoming,
> all ill that shall be,
> I banish away.

Boundaries

The guide or a warder circles the ritual area clockwise, bearing a staff, while saying:

> Sunwise I walk the way of wonder
> with sacred staff the worlds I sunder,

as I ride this circle round,
by wit and will may it be bound.

Balance

The guide or another member of the team stands before the high seat and points north, south, east, and west.

Nordhri and Sudhri, Austri and Vestri,
dwarves in all directions dwelling,
honored ones, the earth upholding,
ward us as we work our magic.

"The Summoning Song"

This is a call-and-response song, in which one or more singers sing the first verse, to which the other participants respond with "A horn blows clear from o'er the mountain." Then there is the second verse to which they respond, "And mist rises on the meadow." See page 238 for the sheet music.

Singer: Make plain the path to where we are,

All: A horn calls clear from o'er the mountain,

Singer: The gods to gladden from afar,

All: And mist rises on the meadow.

Singer: The gods to gladden us below,

All: A horn calls clear from o'er the mountain,

Singer: The crashing tides, they ebb and flow,

All: And mist rises on the meadow.

Singer: The crashing tides, against the shore,

All: A horn calls clear from o'er the mountain,

Singer: Nine giant maids a spirit bore,

All: And mist rises on the meadow.

Singer: Nine giant maids a spirit bring,

All: A horn calls clear from o'er the mountain,

Singer: The huldfolk dance round stony ring,

All: And mist rises on the meadow.

Singer: The huldfolk dance to fiddler's tune,

All: A horn calls clear from o'er the mountain,

Singer: Misshapen forms against the moon,

All: And mist rises on the meadow.

Singer: In moonlit night we join their song,

All: A horn calls clear from o'er the mountain,

Singer: Their spun enchantments linger on,

All: And mist rises on the meadow.

Singer: We shriek and dance atop the roofs,

All: A horn calls clear from o'er the mountain,

Singer: While beating drums resound like hooves,

All: And mist rises on the meadow.

Singer: The hounds and eight-legg'd horse we hear,

All: A horn calls clear from o'er the mountain,

Singer: The heart beats quick as Ygg draws near,

All: And mist rises on the meadow.

Singer: An Old One hangs on windswept ash,

All: A horn calls clear from o'er the mountain,

Singer: From darkened eye the lightnings flash,

All: And mist rises on the meadow.

Singer: From Vana-maid old spells we know,

All: A horn calls clear from o'er the mountain,

Singer: By midnight fires her aprons glow,

All: And mist rises on the meadow.

Singer: In feather skins through worlds she flies,

All: A horn calls clear from o'er the mountain,

Singer: In might and lust the Craft she plies,

All: And mist rises on the meadow.

Singer: A shining Dwarf-jewel on her breast,

All: A horn calls clear from o'er the mountain,

Singer: The blood-moist altars Dísir bless't,

All: And mist rises on the meadow.

Singer: To dis and álf an off'ring pour,

All: A horn calls clear from o'er the mountain,

Singer: And whisper open mound's dark door,

All: And mist rises on the meadow.

Singer: The Völva speaks within the mound,

All: A horn calls clear from o'er the mountain,

Singer: Words of wisdom, wyrd unwound,

All: And mist rises on the meadow.

Singer: The old ones sheltered her below,

All: A horn calls clear from o'er the mountain,

Singer: All their ancient Lore to know,

All: And mist rises on the meadow.

Singer: Beneath the earth, the dark queen waits,

All: A horn calls clear from o'er the mountain,

Singer: Only the wise may pass her gates,

All: And mist rises on the meadow.

Singer: Into her home she welcomes all,

All: A horn calls clear from o'er the mountain,

Singer: The world's hope bides within her hall,

All: And mist rises on the meadow.

Singer: Maurnir ancient in Caverns cold,

All: A horn calls clear from o'er the mountain,

Singer: Telling tales of times of old,

All: And mist rises on the meadow.

Singer: Dark Well of Space where fate is laid,

All: A horn calls clear from o'er the mountain,

Singer: From Ice and Fire the worlds are made,

All: And mist rises on the meadow.

Singer: Make plain the path to where we are,

All: A horn calls clear from o'er the mountain,

Singer: The gods to gladden from afar,

All: And mist rises on the meadow.

The guide faces the people.

> **Guide:** Upon this ground the folk are gathered,
> for Heimdall's kin this hall/holt we have hallowed.
> Here is Utgard, outside understanding,
> and Innangard, Midgard's secret center—
> the Way of Wyrd now may we wander.
> Behold, we bide between the worlds!

Invocations

The guide asks the blessing of Freyja, Mistress of Magic, who taught seidh to Odin, upon the working with these words or his or her own:

> Freyja, Freyja, Fair One, hear us,
> Gythja, guide us well this day,
> Vanadis, reveal the vision,
> as to Odin you opened the way.
> Freyja, Freyja, Fair One, follow,
> In thy falcon form wing free!
> Ottar's rider, fate's road show us,
> With Seidhr-sight we now must see!
> Freyja, be welcome.

All: Hail Freyja.

The guide then calls upon Odin, the god of ecstasy and seeker of wisdom, with these words or his or her own:

> Holy Odin, hail to the High One!
> Wanderer, the way through the worlds we would win.
> Rider of Yggdrasil, release the spirit,
> that we may safely fare within.
> Hroptatyr, hidden things revealing,
> Truthfinder, free us now from fear.
> Gagnrath, goodly counsel grant us,
> For all awaiting wisdom here!
> Odin, be welcome!

All: Hail Odin!

The guide or one of the team honors Hella and asks her blessing as the group seeks her realm.

> Queen of Darkness, Loki's daughter,
> Hella, we would seek thy hallows.
> Bless us with thy bright face, lady,
> Show a pathway through the shadows.
> Where the ancestors are waiting,

Seeking answers, we would fare.
For the seers we seek safe passage,
Grant them ward and welcome there.
Hail Hella.

All: Hail Hella!

The guide or one of the team honors the ancestors who we will be visiting.

Our Mighty Mothers here we honor:
whose bodies birthed and souls inspired us
from womb to womb, since world's beginning,
and Fathers of the flesh and spirit,
Sacred seed itself renewing,
Honor we the holy heroes—
alfar and dísir, guard your descendants
upon the road to Hella's home.
Hail the alfar and dísir.

All: Hail the alfar and dísir.

The guide invokes the Norns to bless the work.

Guide: 'Tis time to sing at the Seat of Thul,
at the Well of Urdh to welcome wisdom.
Norns now we summon, for need is upon us,
to foresee what fate has fashioned—
what has been, what is being and becoming.
Be there truth in our seeing, truth in our saying,
understanding in the ears that hear!
Bestowers of blessings, from our words breed good fortune.

II. Spae

If the seers wish to invoke their allies with power songs, they may do so here.

Journey to Helheim

Each guide should work out his or her own version of this journey, being careful to include directions and major landmarks, and returning to them in reverse order on the journey back. Use images that appeal to all the senses. If you wish to use this one, begin with the standard induction introduced in the Journey to Delphi in Chapter II of Part Two (see pages 168 to 169). Then continue with the following:

> At last you see a circle of brightness.
> As you draw closer, you glimpse a broad plain,
> varied with meadow and stream and woodland,
> the Plane of Midgard that lies within.
> A great tree rises in its center.
> This is Yggdrasil, axis of all the worlds—
> so high its branches brush the heavens,
> so wide you can scarcely see around it.

> (The guide selects the desired direction and reads the appropriate description.)

> Three great roots plunge through the soil.
> Beneath the nearest is an opening—
> the root is polished and the stones beneath it worn
> by the passage of many feet.
> This way lies the path to the Underworld
> and the worlds that lie below.

> Bend, and pass beneath the arch.
> A dim, featureless light shows you the way.
> From the north, behind you,
> the dank mists of Niflheim swirl across the path;
> you can hear the bubbling of Hvergelmir,
> from which run all the rivers of all the worlds.
> Pass onward and inward—
> The shades of Svartalfheim cloud your sight,
> but you fare onward;
> the ring of dwarf-hammers grows louder and then fades.

> The way leads down, down and around to the eastward.
> From the roots of the moist mountains of Jotunheim
> fall icy streams.

You come to the river Slith, in whose leaden waters
all the weapons of all the worlds' wars clatter and clank along.
Leap over it and continue onward,
through the Ironwood where howling, the wild wargs roam.

Down and around, down to the south you pass,
where the air grows hot and dry,
and the fires of Muspel sear the air.
Through the charred trunks of Myrkwood you make your way,
past the river of blood that rises to your knee.

And down and around, down and around
to the west lies your way,
where the Thunderflood comes roaring down,
and beneath the second great root of the Tree
you glimpse the Well of Wyrd and the judgment seats of the gods.

Yet still you must fare onward,
around to the north once more.
The way grows steep. Below, you see a stone tower.
As you approach, a maiden of giant size comes forth,
armed and holding a spear.
She bars the way.
This is Modgudh, who challenges all who take this path.
She stops you and asks,
"Who are you, and why have you come here?"
And in the silence of your heart, you find an answer . . .

(Pause)

When you have answered, Modgudh stands aside.
The way is clear before you—
below, you can hear the roar of a mighty river,
the river Gjoll, deep in its gorge.
One bridge only arches across it,
so bright that it seems thatched with gold.
To the one who fares boldly,

it seems broad and fair.
To the one who fares with fear,
it is sharp as the blade of a sword.
Go forward, as need compels you,
and seek the other side.

The wall that surrounds Hella's home curves away before you.
On the other side you can hear a cock crowing.
There are apple orchards here, and the green hemlock grows.
Follow the wall around to the eastward,
ahead and around, until you come to the eastern gate.
Strong are its pillars and mighty its timbers,
bound with iron, graven over with runes of power.
Here we will wait—all but one—
one soul only may pass within.

(Stop drumming)

Seer, the journey is completed. The gate stands before us.
Will you enter Hella's kingdom to see for the people?

First Seer: I will.

If the first seer has not already ascended, he or she takes her seat. If the first seer narrated the journey, another now takes over as guide.

Guide: All hail to thy going, all hail to thy coming,
all hail to thee, hence and hither.
See the gate before you—for you only, it will swing open.
Our love will go with you,
the silver cord connects us,
your allies will show you the way.
Go in now—see the gate opening.

The guide leads the singing of the "Passage Song" (see page 239) three to five times.

The guide continues to lead singing and drumming while observing the seer. When he or she senses that the seer is in deep trance, the singing and drumming stops.

> **Guide:** [Names self] I hight, through worlds have I wandered,
> Seeking the seer whom now I summon—
> by blood and bone, by stock and stone;
> by time and tide, by waters wide;
> by breath and breeze, by fire that frees,
> come to my summoning!
> [Name, Name], Wise One, witness,
> From depths of darkness where thou art dreaming:
> Dost thou hear me?
>
> (Wait for response)
>
> Tell us what thou dost see.

The seer is allowed time to describe the scene, which helps to complete his or her transition.

> **Guide:** The spell is spoken, the Seer awaits.
> Is there one here who would ask a question?

Those who have questions raise their hands, and the guide points to one of them.

The first querent asks a question. (Depending on the size of the group, he or she may need to stand or come forward.)

> **Guide:** Cease not seer, 'til said thou hast,
> answer the asker till all he (or she) knows.

The seer searches for an answer. When it is finished, he or she says something like,

> Wit ye more, or how?
>
> (or)
>
> This thou dost know. Would'st thou know more?

Here the querent may ask the seer for more information or ask a related question.

When the answer is completed and accepted, the guide says:

> Well have you asked and well been answered.
> Is there another who has a question?

The next questioner speaks, and procedure is repeated.

When the first seer has answered enough questions, the guide says:

> The hour grows late, the people weary,
> It is time to return to where we are waiting.
> Turn now, can you see the gate?
> Come back to us now.

The guide can pull on the "silver cord" or direct the seer to look for his or her power animal, who will lead the way back. If the seer is resistant, the guide will need to "talk the seer down," rather as ground control does for a pilot. If necessary, the guide should call the seer's magical name and ask that persona to give way to the mundane person. In emergencies, the guide can send his or her own power animal in after the seer, or go him- or herself.

When the guide senses that the seer is through, he or she describes the gate shutting behind him. Warders help the seer down from the high seat. Someone should watch over him or her until he or she is grounded. If there are more questions and another seer is available, the guide may continue:

> But still the people wait for wisdom.
> Who else will dare the gate of darkness?

The second seer answers, "I will." The warders help him or her into the high seat.

> **Guide:** All hail to thy going! all hail to thy coming!
> All hail to thee, hence and hither!

Repeat the procedure for questioning, summoning the seer back, and singing a new seer through the gate. When all questions have been answered (or you are out of time), the guide brings the last seer through the gates and narrates the homeward journey.

> The gate is shut, and we are together.
> It is time now to return to the upper world.
> Together we will fare, together we will ascend,
> swiftly and safely until we are in Midgard once more.

> Move now along the path that leads beside the wall.
> Before you is the bridge over the river Gjoll, broad and fair.
> You cross, and take the trail upward, filled with energy,
> past Modgudh's tower.
> Up and around, up and around you fare,
> from the north to the west,
> past the Thunderflood and the Well of Wyrd.

> Up and around, up and around once more,
> through the hot, bright air of Muspelheim that burns in the south
> and around to the east where the streams of Jotunheim come
> down.
> Up and around, up and around,
> come back to the north again,
> passing through Svartalfheim's shadows
> and the mists of Niflheim.

> And now you see the arching root
> and the bright glimmer of Midgard that lies within.
> Pass under the root and up to the trunk of the Tree.
> This is your center, the center of all worlds.

From here, bring participants back to consensus consciousness using the standard closing induction introduced in the Journey to Delphi in Part Two, Chapter II (see the italicized text on pages 171 to 172). Then the guide or another member of the team sing the verses of the "Returning Song" (see page 240), and everyone joins in the chorus.

> **Guide:** Now the vision vanishes.
> The spirit voice is still.

The body's bonds do draw you back
with wisdom ruled by will.

All: The way that you did learn
we call you to return.

Guide: Odin utters now the word
that well shall ward your way.
Sleipnir swiftly bears you back
from darkness into day.

All: The way that you did learn
we call you to return . . .

Guide: Freyja's falcon-dress shall find
you wings if you have need.
Swiftly fly and safely fare,
return to us with speed.

All: The way that you did learn
we call you to return.

Guide: Behold your bodies patient wait
to welcome well your souls,
Sink down and enter safely in,
For now you are made whole.

All: The way that you did learn
we call you to return . . .

III. Returning to the World

Those who invoked the alfar and dísir, Hella, Odin, and Freyja
thank them. The dwarves are also thanked by the one who invoked
them.

> Nordhri and Sudhri, Austri and Vestri,
> dwarves in all directions dwelling,
> honored ones, the earth upholding,
> continue to uphold it, nice and steady.

Guide: Round about and back again,
Sacred circle be undone—
this place to all good use returned,
leave us with the lore we've learned.

As the ritual concludes, warders make sure that everyone is back to consensus consciousness.

AN APPENDIX OF SONGS

Hallowed Well of Wisdom

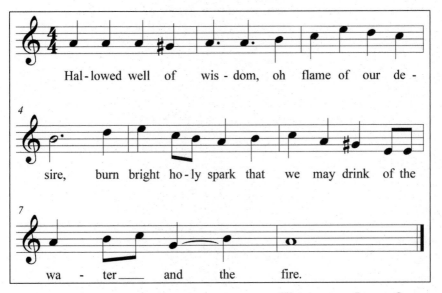

Hal-lowed well of wis-dom, oh flame of our desire, burn bright ho-ly spark that we may drink of the
wa - ter___ and the fire.

WORDS, MUSIC, LAUREL OLSON

Veil Song

Be - hind the veil you go, wis-dom's way to show, speed on - ward, seer, fare wi - thout fear, 'till all we need___ we know....

WORDS, MUSIC, DIANA L. PAXSON

This We Know

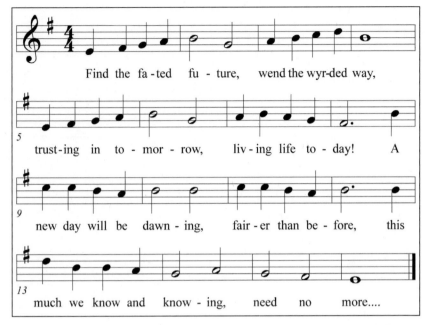

Find the fa-ted fu - ture, wend the wyr-ded way,
trust-ing in to - mor - row, liv - ing life to - day! A
new day will be dawn - ing, fair - er than be - fore, this
much we know and know - ing, need no more....

WORDS, MUSIC, DIANA L. PAXSON

Spindle Song

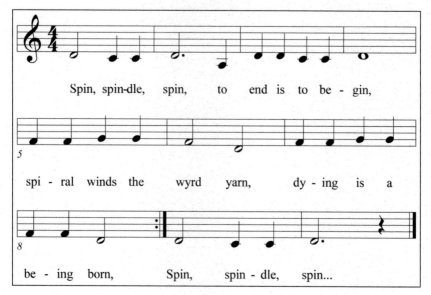

Spin, spin-dle, spin, to end is to be - gin,

spi - ral winds the wyrd yarn, dy - ing is a

be - ing born, Spin, spin - dle, spin...

WORDS, MUSIC, LEIGH ANN HUSSEY

Holy Three

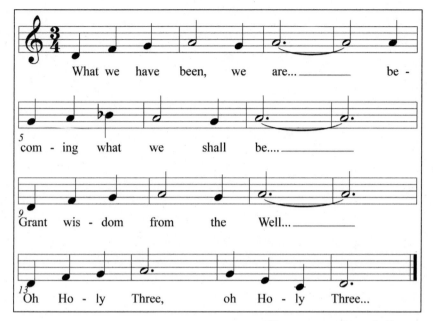

What we have been, we are... be -
com - ing what we shall be....
Grant wis - dom from the Well...
Oh Ho - ly Three, oh Ho - ly Three...

WORDS, MUSIC, DIANA L. PAXSON

Paean

Pae - an pae - an ho - ly A - pol - lon,

de - scend in wind and fire...

Pae - an pae - an ho - ly A - pol - lon,

our spi - rits in - spire...

1.Dark ___ the world, ___ dark and wi - thout mo - tion,
2.Hear the tree-tops shi - ver, the ve - ry air is thrum-ming,
3.Of a sud-den, bright-ness bla - zes in high hea - ven,
4.Di - vine One we pray Thee, grant our spi - rits cour - age,

when the sun is hid - den, cold, and nothing grows.
see the sha-dows shim - mer, a cres - cent of fine gold
blin - ding the sen - ses as the pure spirit soars;
clear sighted to per - cieve wi - thin Thy cleansing rays

Dark - er man's spirit when the holy flame is ab sent, __
ar - ches __ in fire a - bove the far ho - ri - zon, the
far - see - ing swift striding, glo - ri - ous A - pol-lon, ap-
that per-fection of Beau - ty which in Thy Mind lives ev-er, and

__ dull and life - less until divine wind blows.
god's bow __ bends, light shoots a - cross the world!
pears in __ splen - dour as the world a - dores!
give us the skill to trans - form it into praise!

WORDS, MUSIC, DIANA L. PAXSON

The Summoning Song

Make plain the path to where we are.

A horn calls clear from o'er the moun - tain,

the gods to glad - den from a - far,

and mist ri - ses on the mea - dow...

Lyrics by Konradr Trollmadhr and Alfredr Ingvisson
Music adapted from "Heimo og Nykkjen"

Passage Song

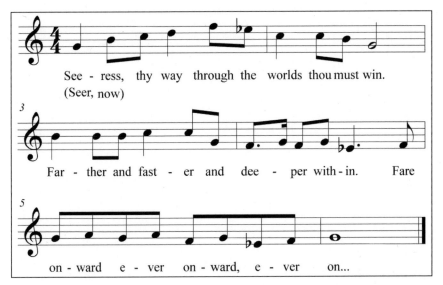

See - ress, thy way through the worlds thou must win.
(Seer, now)

Far - ther and fast - er and dee - per with - in. Fare

on - ward e - ver on - ward, e - ver on...

LYRICS BY DIANA L. PAXSON
MUSIC ADAPTED FROM "STOLI OLI"

Returning Song

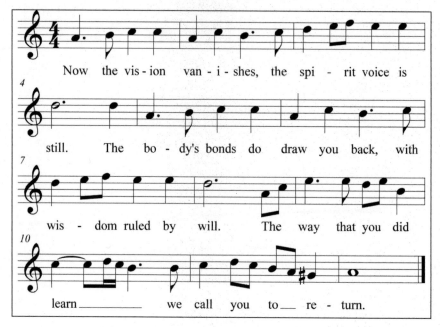

Now the vis-ion van-i-shes, the spi-rit voice is still. The bo-dy's bonds do draw you back, with wis-dom ruled by will. The way that you did learn____ we call you to__ re-turn.

LYRICS BY DIANA L. PAXSON
MUSIC ADAPTED FROM "MARGIT OG TARGJEI RISVOLLO"

BIBLIOGRAPHY

Adhalsteinsson, Jón Hnefil. *Under the Cloak: The Acceptance of Christianity in Iceland with Particular Reference to the Religious Attitudes Prevailing at the Time*. Reykjavik: Háskólútgáfan Félagsvísindastofnun, 1999.

Aeschylus. *Agamemnon*. Edited by Charles W. Eliot. Translated by E. D. A. Morshead. Vol. 8, Part 1 of The Harvard Classics. New York: P. F. Collier & Son, 1909–14.

———. *The Eumenides*. Translated by A. W. Verrall. London: MacMillan & Co., 1908.

Babbage, Charles. *Passages from the Life of a Philosopher*. London: Longman, Green, Longman, Roberts & Green. 1864.

Bauschatz, Paul C. *The Well and the Tree: World and Time in Early Germanic Culture*. Amherst: University of Massachusetts Press, 1982.

Blain, Jenny. *Nine Worlds of Seid-Magic: Ecstasy and Neo-Shamanism in North European Paganism*. London: Routledge, 2002.

Braude, Ann. *Radical Spirits: Spiritualism and Women's Rights in Nineteenth-Century America*. Bloomington: Indiana University Press, 2001.

Broad, William J. *The Oracle: The Lost Secrets and Hidden Messages of Ancient Delphi*. New York: Penguin Books, 2006.

Brodribb, William Jackson. *Tacitus, Annals*. New York: Modern Library, 1942.

Callimachus. *Callimachus: Hymns and Epigrams, Lycophron and Aratus*. Translated by A. W. Mair and G. R. Mair. Vol. 129 of Loeb Classical Library. London: William Heinemann, 1921.

Cleasby, Richard, and Guðbrandur Vigfússon. *Icelandic–English Dictionary*. Oxford: Clarendon Press, LXXIV.

Davidson, Hilda Ellis, ed. *The Seer in Celtic and Other Traditions*. Edinburgh: John Donald Publishers, 1989.

Dempsey, T. *The Delphic Oracle: Its Early History, Influence and Fall*. Oxford: Blackwell, 1918.

Dioscorides, Pedanius. *De Materia Medica*. Translated by Lily Y. Beck. Hildesheim, Germany: Olms-Weidmann, 2005.

Dobin, Howard. *Merlin's Disciples: Prophecy, Poetry, and Power in Renaissance England*. Stanford, CA: Stanford University Press, 1990.

Eliade, Mircea. *Shamanism: Archaic Techniques of Ecstasy*. Translated by Willard R. Trask. New York: Bollingen Foundation, 1964.

Ellis, Hilda Roderick. *The Road to Hel: A Study of the Conception of the Dead in Old Norse Literature*. Cambridge, U.K.: Cambridge University Press, 1943.

Euripides. *Ion*. Translated by A. W. Verrall. Cambridge, U.K.: Cambridge University Press, 1890.

Evans, W. H. *How to be a Medium*. Philadelphia: David McKay Co., c. 1950.

Fielding, Charles, and Carr Collins. *The Story of Dion Fortune*. Dallas: Star & Cross, 1985.

Flowers, Stephen E., and James A. Chisholm, eds. and trans. *A Sourcebook of Seidh*. Smithville, TX: Runa-Raven, 2002.

Fontenrose, Joseph. *The Delphic Oracle: Its Responses and Operations*. Berkeley: University of California Press, 1978, 1981.

Fortune, Dion. *Moon Magic*. York Beach, ME: Samuel Weiser, 1978.

Fox, Robin Lane. *Pagans and Christians*. San Francisco: Harper San Francisco, 1986.

Giubelli, Giorgio. *Phlegrean Fields*. Napoli, Italy: Carcavallo Editore, 1997.

Gunnell, Terry. *The Origins of Drama in Scandinavia*. New York: Boydell and Brewer, 1995.

Harner, Michael. *The Way of the Shaman*. New York: Harper & Row, 1980.

Herodotus. *The Histories of Herodotus*. Translated by C. E. Godley. Cambridge, MA: Harvard University Press, Loeb Classical Library, 1920.

Høst, Annette. "The Staff and the Song: Using the Old Nordic Seidr in Modern Shamanism." Scandinavian Center for Shamanic Studies. Last updated July 18, 2011. *www.shamanism.dk/Artikel - THE STAFF AND THE SONG.htm*.

Iamblichus. *Theurgia: or, The Egyptian Mysteries*. Translated by Alexander Wilder. London: William Rider & Son Ltd., 1911.

James, William. *William James on Psychical Research*. Compiled and edited by Gardner Murphy, MD, and Robert O. Ballou. New York: Viking Press, 1960.

Lang, Andrew. "Discussion of the Trance Phenomena of Mrs. Piper." In *Proceedings of the Society for Psychical Research*. Vol. 15. Society for Psychical Research. London: Kegan Paul, Trench, Trübner & Co., 1901.

Leto, Steven. "Magical Potions: Entheogenic Themes in Scandinavian Mythology." *Shaman's Drum* 54 (2000): 55–65.

Little, William. *The Psychic Tourist: A Voyage into the Curious World of Predicting the Future*. London: Icon Books, 2009.

Loewe, Michael, and Carmen Blacker, eds. *Oracles and Divination*. Boulder, CO: Shambhala Publications, 1981.

Luhrmann, Tanya. *Persuasions of the Witch's Craft: Ritual Magic in Contemporary England*. Cambridge, MA: Harvard University Press, 1989.

Matthews, John, ed. *The Celtic Seers' Sourcebook: Vision and Magic in the Druid Tradition*. London: Blandford Press, 1999.

———. *The Druid Source Book*. London: Blandford Press, 1996.

May, Jo. *Fogou: A Journey into the Underworld*. Glastonbury: Gothic Image, 1996.

McLaren, Karla. "Bridging the Chasm between Two Cultures." *Skeptical Inquirer* 28, no. 3 (May 2004).

Merriam-Webster Online, www.merriam-webster.com.

Oates, Whitney J, and Eugene O'Neill, Jr., eds. *The Complete Greek Drama*. Vol. 1, *Ion* by Euripides, trans. Robert Potter. New York: Random House, 1938. (Available online at the Perseus Project, www.perseus.tufts.edu/hopper/text?doc=Perseus:text:1999.01.0110.)

Osterreich, T. K. *Possession*. New Hyde Park, NY: University Books, 1966.

Pausanias. *Guide to Greece, Vol. I: Central Greece*. Translated by Peter Levi. London: Penguin Books, 1971.

Paxson, Diana L. "In the Fields of Fire." *Sagewoman* (Fall 1998).

———. *Trance-Portation: Learning to Navigate the Inner World*. San Francisco: Red Wheel/Weiser, 2008.

Peyser, Randy. "Bay Area Psychics: Three Profiles." www.randypeyser.com/3profiles.htm.

Phillpotts, Bertha. *The Elder Edda and Ancient Scandinavian Drama*. Cambridge, U.K.: Cambridge University Press, 1920.

Plato. *Phaedrus*. Translated by Benjamin Jowett. Internet Classics Archive, classics.mit.edu/Plato/phaedrus.html.

Plutarch. *Moralia, Vol V. De Defectu Oraculae*, and *Why the Pythia Does not Now Give Oracles in Verse*. Translated by Frank Coel Babbitt. Loeb Classical Library. Cambridge, MA: Harvard University Press, 1936.

————. *De Morialia VI, On Talkativeness.* Translated by W. C. Helmbold. Loeb Classical Library. Cambridge, MA: Harvard University Press, 1939.

The Poetic Edda. Vol. III: Mythological Poems. Edited and translated by Ursula Dronke. Oxford: Clarendon Press, 1997.

The Poetic Edda. Translated by Lee M. Hollander. Austin: University of Texas, 1986.

Price, Neil. *The Viking Way: Religion and War in Late Iron Age Scandinavia.* Uppsala, Sweden: Department of Archaeology and Ancient History, University of Uppsala, 2002.

Raine, Kathleen, and George Mills Harper, eds. *Thomas Taylor the Platonist: Selected Writings.* Princeton, NJ: Princeton University Press, 1969.

Rees, Alwin and Brinley. *Celtic Heritage.* London: Thames & Hudson, 1961.

Ross, Anne. *Pagan Celtic Britain.* New York: Columbia University Press, 1967.

Runic, John. *The Book of Seidr.* Milverton, U.K.: Capall Bann Publishing, 2004.

The Saga of Erik the Red, translated by Keneva Kunz. In *The Sagas of Icelanders.* London: Penguin, 2001.

Saxo Grammaticus. *Gesta Danorum.* Translated by Peter Fisher. Edited by H. R. Ellis Davidson. Cambridge, U.K. D. S. Brewer, 1979.

Shakespeare, William. *As You Like It.* The New Folger Library Shakespeare. New York: Simon & Schuster, 2004.

Skafte, Dianne. *When Oracles Speak.* Wheaton, IL: Quest Books, 2000.

Smith, Daniel B. *Muses, Madmen, and Prophets.* New York: The Penguin Press, 2007.

Snorri, Sturlusson. *Edda*. Translated by Anthony Faulkes. London: J. M. Dent & Sons, 1987.

———. *Heimskringla*. New York: Dover, 1932, 1990.

Sophocles. *Oedipus the King*. Translated by F. Storr. London: William Heineman, 1912.

Spence, Lewis. *Second Sight, Its History and Origins*. London: Rider & Co., 1951.

Spenser, Edmund. *The Faerie Queene*. London: William Ponsonbie, 1596.

Sutherland, Elizabeth. *Ravens and Black Rain*. London: Constable, 1985.

Tacitus. *The Complete Works of Tacitus*. Edited by Moses Hadas. New York: Modern Library, 1942.

Tain Bo Cuailnge. Translated by Thomas Kinsella. Oxford: Oxford University Press, 1969.

Tart, Charles T., ed. *Altered States of Consciousness*. 3rd edition. San Francisco: Harper San Francisco, 1990.

Taylor, Jill Bolte. "Jill Bolte Taylor's Stroke of Insight." Interactive transcript. TED, Ideas Worth Spreading. posted March, 2008. *www.ted.com/talks/jill_bolte_taylor_s_powerful_stroke_of_insight.html#*.

Temple, Robert. *Oracles of the Dead*. Rochester, VT: Destiny Books, 2005.

Thurston, Herbert. "This Rock." *Catholic Answers* (March 1995).

Vandenberg, Philipp. *Mysteries of the Oracles: The Last Secrets of Antiquity*. London: Tauris Parke Paperbacks, 2007.

Viga-Glum's Saga, with the Tales of Ogmund Bash and Thorvald Chatterbox. Translated by John McKinnell. Edinburgh: Canongate, 1972.

Virgil. *The Aeneid of Virgil*. Translated by Allen Mandelbaum. New York: Bantam, 1961.

Wallace, Robert J. *Shamans/Neo-Shamans*. London: Routledge, 2003.

Wier, Dennis R. *Trance, from Magic to Technology*. Ann Arbor, MI: Trans Media, 1996.

ABOUT THE AUTHOR

DIANA L. PAXSON was raised in California. After graduating from Mills College and receiving an M.S. from the University of California, she wrote educational materials before beginning a career as a novelist, resulting in 29 novels and 75 short stories, including the Avalon series (writing for Marion Zimmer Bradley) and the *Chronicles of Westria*. While a graduate student in Berkeley she started the Society for Creative Anachronism.

In the eighties Diana became active in the evolving pagan movement, founding a women's spirituality circle with Marion Zimmer Bradley, and later the Fellowship of the Spiral Path. She was ordained as a priestess in 1982. From 1990 to 1991 she served as First Officer of the Covenant of the Goddess. During the '90s her focus began to shift to Asatru (Norse paganism). In 1992 she joined the Troth, an international Asatru organization, in which she is an Elder and has served as a board member and Steerswoman (chair).

In addition to writing, Diana teaches regular classes in runelore and trance work. She has been a presenter at many conferences and festivals. She currently directs the Troth's clergy training program and edits its magazine, *Idunna*. Her work with the runes resulted in her book *Taking Up the Runes* (Weiser, 2005). Her study of trance work resulted in the book *Trance-Portation* (Weiser, 2008). Her pioneering work in recovering of techniques for the Viking-Age practice of oracular seidh is presented in the book you are holding in your hands.

She lives in Berkeley, California.

ALSO BY DIANA PAXSON

Trance-Portation: Learning to Navigate the Inner World

Essential Asatru: Walking the Path of Norse Paganism

Taking Up the Runes: A Complete Guide to Using Runes in Spells, Rituals, Divination, and Magic

Celestial Wisdom for Every Year of Your Life: Discover the Hidden Meaning of Your Age (with Z. Budapest)

For a complete list of Diana Paxson's fiction and non-fiction work, please visit *www.diana-paxson.com*.

For more information on her Oracular practice, visit *www.seidh.org*.

TO OUR READERS